THE PERFECT EGG
AND OTHER SECRETS

THE PERFECT EGG AND OTHER SECRETS

by

Aldo Buzzi

*Recipes, curiosities, secrets of high- and low-brow
cookery, from watered salad to boarding-house*
pastina in brodo, *from Apicius to Michel Guérard,
from Alexandre Dumas to Carlo Emilio Gadda, from
the Curé de Bregnier to St Nikolaus von Flüe*

Translated from the Italian by Guido Waldman

With fourteen drawings by Saul Steinberg

BLOOMSBURY

The translator is hugely grateful to his Roman sister,
Jehanne-Marie Marchesi, for resolving a number of
linguistic perplexities in the culinary field.

The publishers gratefully acknowledge Ponte alle Grazie
for their permission to reproduce a number of passages.

Drawings by Saul Steinberg © The Saul Steinberg
Foundation/Artists Rights Society (ARS) New York. The
fourteen drawings represent works, or photocopies of works,
that Steinberg sent to Buzzi from the 1950s on.

Published by Bloomsbury Publishing, New York and London
Distributed to the trade by Holtzbrinck Publishers

All papers used by Bloomsbury Publishing are natural,
recyclable products made from wood grown in well-managed
forests. The manufacturing processes conform to the
environmental regulations of the country of origin.

Library of Congress Cataloging-in-Publication Data
has been applied for.

ISBN 1-58234-604-6
ISBN-13 978-1-58234-604-5

First U.S. edition 2005

1 3 5 7 9 10 8 6 4 2

Typeset by Hewer Text Ltd, Edinburgh
Printed in the United States of America
by Quebecor World Fairfield

'Me, I like my pancake broad but thick.'

Traveller on the Milan–Bergamo line

CONTENTS

PART TWO

PART ONE

Sopa de lima

It was a fine spring day, the sky was the colour
of blotting paper. It was hot, one might have
been out there ... at Mérida, in Yucatán
(Mexico). I crossed the hotel patio; in the middle
of the lawn there was the pretence of a well,
with two large parrots perched on it the whole
time, too many colours by half. Out in the
sun-dazzled road, with the short, black shadows
of midday, I stopped a carriage, a very narrow
thing (it existed only in profile), and had it take
me to the Dos Tulipancitos, the best restaurant
in town. Its speciality was *sopa de lima*, lime
soup, a delectable, light soup, a feast for the
eyes, and, although served hot, just the ticket
even in the tropical heat. The *lima* is a miniature
tropical lemon, perfectly round and the size of a
golf ball, green like a frog, full of juice, and it
doesn't taste like a lemon. *Lima*, plural *lime*, is
the Italian word for the Spanish *lima*, plural
limas, and the English lime, plural limes. As
the prime meaning of *lima* (and generally the
only one given in Italian dictionaries) is that
of the well-known metal utensil, the idea of a

lima soup is, at first blush, a repulsive absurdity.[1]

For years I've been wanting another taste of *sopa de lima*. But it is not easy: above all limes are not readily available; they are only to be found now and then at a high-class greengrocer's. Limes are used in making daiquiris – if lemon is used the result is a fake daiquiri.

To obtain the recipe I try writing to Carletto Tibón, whom I knew back then in Mexico City; he it was who had suggested the soup to me when I had gone for a (delicious) meal at his house. Years have passed, and Tibón has retired to Cuernavaca.

Dear Signor Buzzi,

I have your message: If I were kind, I should say I remember you well. But alas no, not even that there were three of you when you went to make a film in Yucatán. Patellani, a Genoese *marchese*, and the lady, Lattuada, the sister of our good friend.[2] What about you? Do send me a photograph to reawaken my flagging memory. Your visit must go back dozens of years, when my

[1] The author plays on the similarity of the Spanish word for lime with the Italian word for a file or rasp, and briefly embroiders on this. The Italian (Sicilian) word for the fruit is in fact *lumia*. (Translator)

[2] Patellani is Count Federico, one of the best-known Lombard photographers and journalists of our day, and the lady is the sister of the film/stage director Alberto Lattuada.

4

mother was still alive – she came here from Monte Olimpino (Cardina) in 1956. [. . .]

As for the *sopa de lima*, I shall try to obtain the recipe from some Yucatán folk and add it at the end of this letter. I have tasted it: it is light and flavoursome. But what about the limes? We always used to get them from Sicily and from Rossano in Calabria: from the first crop, in November if I'm not mistaken. The tortillas, which are cut into thin strips, can easily be replaced by strips of pancake; in Austria they make a broth and cut in strips of omelette. Here the tortilla is done in a roll (*taco*), then sliced. However, coming to the soup you're asking about, the tortilla is fried in oil until crisp. In Italy you might settle for potato chips or slices of toast.

Here, now, is the recipe:

Chicken breasts are cooked in salted water with onion and garlic.

Small cubes of tomato are fried and tossed into the broth, to colour it, along with slices of bitter lime.

Once the chicken breasts are cooked, they are cut into thin slices.

The strips of tortilla are fried (toasted).

The onions, limes and garlic are removed from the broth.

The strips of chicken and tortilla are put into soup bowls and the broth is poured over them.

Serve with limes cut in two, which guests may squeeze into the soup as required.

I think that in Italy you might use only one or two limes for the broth, then add lemon juice.

That's all I can tell you. I know a little about cooking, but it's all theory: in practice I'm pretty useless.

With fondest greetings.

My reply evoked a further reply from Tibón.

Dear Signor Buzzi,

Although your letter absolves me from replying, I am answering nonetheless so as to be able to file it with the previous correspondence.

We did get our limes from Rossano in Calabria.

There was a pharmacist (I believe he was killed by the partisans) called Rizzo Corallo. But you could write and ask the mayor, or even inquire at the Chamber of Commerce at Catania or Palermo, and find out who grows them and who exports them.

In any event, as I think I've told you, *sopa de lima* is not a traditional dish; it was invented in Yucatán but it's been so successful it's now served in every restaurant [. . .] I have written a fair number of recipes for a small fashion paper run by my friends at Garzanti [the Italian publishers]. They were terribly complicated recipes that ended with 'Toss the whole lot into the dustbin and make for the nearest rosticcieria' [. . .]

Warmest greetings from this hot-spot, Cuernavaca.

The limes have arrived. For the broth, instead of potato chips or omelette I have used home-made *piadine romagnole* (thin slabs of unleavened dough enriched with lard) cooked on the griddle and carefully cut into strips a centimetre wide, so that they do not break; then they are toasted on the griddle, without burning them: half a *piadina* per person. And I haven't omitted the small onion cut in two or the two slices of lime. The important thing is that the stock should be extra-special, as it always is in poor countries: like Mexico and the Abruzzi . . . With the advent of Progress the chicken mutates into chicken cubes.

I have made a daiquiri by way of apéritif: a small glass of Bacardi rum carte blanche, the juice of half a lime and a small half-spoonful of sugar shaken up rapidly with ice (dry!) in the shaker and poured into a small crystal goblet that has spent some time in the freezer, its rim abundantly frosted with finely crushed ice. The daiquiri takes on the colour of water that has frozen, with vague yellow-green reflections from the lime juice: a nacreous mother-of-pearl hue ideally as depicted by Manet.

For the *piadine* what is needed is a not-too-fine metal griddle (about one millimetre thick) placed on the fire or gas hob. Those you buy in Romagna are circular, some 30 centimetres in diameter, with two small handles.

For four *piadine*: Take 250 g flour, 25 g lard, a half spoonful of oil (or you can omit the lard and use oil on its own, about two spoonfuls), a pinch of salt, warm water.

Mix the flour, oil and lard in a bowl, adding the water a little at a time. Knead the mixture on the worktop until you have a smooth dough that is not sticky. Divide it into four equal pieces and shape each into a ball. Take one ball, roll it out into a thin, round sheet, lay it on the heated griddle, and prick it with a fork in order to remove any air bubbles as they form. Turn the *piadina* over after a minute, grasping it by the edge, which will magically curl up, and cook it for a minute on the other side. It is eaten like bread, or as the Mexicans eat tortillas, wrapping it round a filling: cheese, ham, cooked vegetables, something spicy . . . whatever your fancy, stimulated by your appetite, may suggest.

Watered Salad

Meat and vegetables. A grilled steak or a *paillard* with salad: a tomato salad seasoned with salt, coarsely ground black pepper and red vinegar (no oil), plus a green salad with a Tuscan dressing consisting simply of oil (olive, of course) and salt.

At this point I proffer a word of advice that tends to be greeted with diffidence and is seldom followed: oil, salt and *a little water*. The water does not dilute the taste of the oil, it serves to bring it out. After washing the salad and giving it a whirl in its wire basket or in a dish towel, don't get rid of all the water; the few drops that remain on the leaves will, along with the oil and salt, provide the perfect dressing (as also for chopped fennel or celery). Serve the two salads thus dressed in two separate salad bowls, and of course eat them together.

When this theory was expounded in an aristocratic London club in Jermyn Street, 'whispered cries' (if this expression will render my meaning) were to be heard issuing from the mouths (those that were empty at that moment) of the diners: 'Unbelievable! That's odd! Ominous! By Jove! Preposterous! . . .'

But once the extra-virgin olive oil had been procured, with some difficulty, and after putting the theory into practice, further 'whispered cries' underlined the general consensus: 'Terrific! Fantastic! Fabulous! My goodness!' . . .

Meat and vegetables again.

'When a man's been slaving away the entire day are you really going to keep feeding him on greens?'

'It's meat you need, meat beefs up your blood.'

'Just imagine! If my husband, God rest his soul, didn't find I'd put meat on his plate every day, he'd slap me all over the face.'

The above dialogue, which doesn't amount to much, comes at the end of Fellini's film *Il Bidone.*

Such idle chatter would have quite escaped Broderick Crawford as he lay dying just beyond the brow of the road along which a group of peasant women walked chatting to one another. Translated into Sardinian and spoken, the exchanges became what they were supposed to be, at once incomprehensible and charged with meaning: the very essence of life, which appears wonderful at last to a person who is about to leave it for good.

'*A un omini che traballa tutu sa santa dì sempri birdura di bolis donai?*'

'*Pezza ci bòlidi, puita sa pezza di rinforza su sànguni.*'

'*Là! Su primu maridu miu bonanima, si no di femmu incontrai sa pezza dogna dì mi prenia savàcc e bussinadas.*'

When the film was shown in Sardinia the effect was lost. Everyone, including the dying man, distinctly heard the women's chatter: 'When a man's been slaving away the entire day are you really going to keep feeding him on greens? It's meat you need . . .'

A *paillard*, as everybody knows, is a thin slice of veal (or of beef, as it was originally, Carnacina recently reminded us), grilled and seasoned with pepper, salt and lemon juice. Monsieur Paillard, once the proprietor of a famous Paris restaurant on the Boulevard des Italiens, and previously chef at the Ritz, has achieved immortality with very little effort – but only in Italy. In France, gastronomically speaking, *paillard* does not convey anything at all: it's as if someone were to ask (Italian-style) for *vitel tonné*.

Avgolémono

The sun had set. Our driver, Mihalis Hanzidiaco, took a rapid turn around the harbour (at Rhodes) to give us a glimpse of the old town.

'And the Colossus?' I asked.

'Only on a postcard.'

The true cause of the collapse of the Colossus, a cause that even today threatens so many other famous monuments with extinction, was pointed out by Ennio Flaiano in his *Diario notturno*. 'It is generally believed that the Colossus of Rhodes collapsed in an earthquake. This is not the whole story. The Colossus of Rhodes collapsed owing to the verbiage that tourists, in addition to their names, scratched into the pedestal and which, increasing over the centuries in number and in vulgarity, undermined its resistance. The earthquake achieved only that little that remained to be done.'

Rhodes is the city of roses. We were passing the old Hôtel des Roses. No scent of roses in the air, but rather the aroma from the thousands of spits and griddles in action in the old quarter and in the new. And to think that Antagoras, the ancient poet of Rhodes, had a weakness for chicken broth!

The countryside was for the most part a place of rocks and stones, with little in the way of dwellings.

'And the valley of the butterflies?' I asked Mihalis.

'They'll be asleep at this hour.'

In the sky, which was now the deepest blue, there hung a thin sickle moon (Turkey is only a few miles off), and where the sun had set there lingered a strong light that was not red but yellow, the magic light of the Orient, and it seemed to be growing. I was still thinking of Antagoras. Only a few verses have survived from his entire œuvre; absolutely nothing from the epic poem *The Thebaid* which is attributed to him. To make up for that, what has survived to our own day, across two dozen centuries, is his nickname: the Glutton. What was his favourite dish? His secret recipe? Perhaps he would have enjoyed the Futurists' rose-petal soup.

After 60 kilometres even the yellow light of Aladdin's lamp had gone out. The car stopped at the side of the road: through the window came the damp smell of the cypresses, the pines, the aromatic herbs.

'From here,' said Mihalis professionally, 'you get the best view of Lindos and its bay.'

All I could see, down below, was the odd light drowned in the utter darkness that alarms anyone looking out at night over the immensity of the sea. The restaurants in Lindos were doing a roaring trade. At the Restaurant Bar Cléobule the clients were sipping Mapolé lemonade and 'miniatures' of ouzo, nibbling at slices of wholemeal bread spread with excellent *taramasalata*. Greek cooking is Balkan cooking, and Balkan cooking is Turkish cooking. The symbol of Turkish cuisine is the meatball, a dish which, as we all know, can be perfection or an abortion and thus is generally regarded with suspicion, as is Bologna mortadella in London: in English, boloney is another word for rubbish.

I overcame my hesitation by ordering, on the advice of a local notable, *avgolémono*: a fish soup rather different from the usual ones, without garlic, without tomato; dreamed up, maybe, by Cleobulus, one of the Seven Sages of antiquity, who was born in Lindos and, after governing the city for forty years, was buried here, so it is said, within a tumbledown monument that may be glimpsed on the far left of the bay: far enough off so that the tourists, and the donkey drivers who convey them incessantly up to the top of the acropolis, cannot disturb its peace. The recipe was given to me by the chef-proprietor Vassilis Mavricos who, like all Rhodians above a certain age, understands Italian and willingly speaks it, thanks to an occupation which, coming as it did after that of the Turks, has generally left a positive memory.

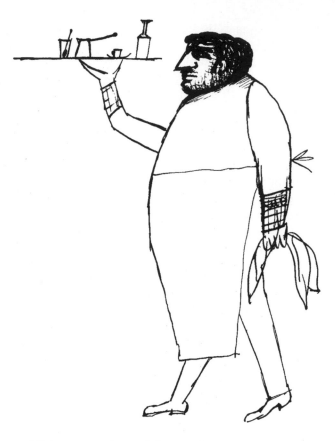

'Take some fatty fish (sea bream or sea bass, etc.), clean them, salt them and leave them to rest while you put the water for the broth into the pot (the water needs to cover the fish well, some two ladlefuls per head) and toss in a whole medium-sized onion and one medium-sized potato, diced, per person, a little carrot, chopped parsley and olive oil. Add salt and bring to the boil.

'When the vegetables start to cook and the oil turns light, drop the fish into the broth along with the juice of half a lemon or more, depending on the quantity of fish. And when the fish, onion, potato and carrots are cooked, remove them from the broth, carefully get rid of the fish-heads and any bones, and keep everything warm.

'Strain the broth into another saucepan. Beat an egg (or two, depending on the quantity of broth) in a bowl with two forks' – this is Vassilis's fixation – 'and beat well. When the egg is good and frothy pour on the juice of half a lemon. Then take a ladleful of broth, hot but not boiling, and pour it gently over the egg, beating the whole time with the two forks.

'Pour the egg mixture a little at a time into the broth (off the heat), stirring well with the ladle. Taste and add more salt, pepper and lemon juice if required, divide the pieces of fish and the vegetables among the soup bowls and pour the broth over them.'

This is Vassilis's recipe. I myself would add cubes of bread fried in oil and I would mash in a little cooked potato to give the soup more substance. (*Avgolémono* can also be made with chicken, kid goat, or veal.)

The round bay, closed off like a swimming pool, sparkles beneath the sun; the sea is flat calm; from the beach come the muffled voices of bathers.

Suddenly the silence is broken by the sound of a loud siren that echoes across the bay as far as the distant tomb of Cleobulus. Instinctively the eye looks up from the plate and turns to the boats and caiques lying motionless at anchor. The sound of the siren, which started so well, ends on a sorry, disjointed, plangent note: it is the bray of a donkey.

Towards evening the sirens (brays) increase: the beasts are hungry: they want their *avgolémono* (a bucket of bran) or their *taramà* (a bucket of dry bread outside the house door), and the harbour wakes up to a non-existent traffic. Then over all there descends, or there should descend, the silence of night while in the west Aladdin's yellow lamp is lit.

Taramasalata is made by pounding in a mortar cod's roe, boiled potato, oil, lemon juice, onion and garlic. The result is a soft paste that is spread thickly, as already noted, on slices of wholemeal bread.

Mapolé lemonade is bottled lemonade with an exquisitely natural flavour. The name is made up of the initial letters of mandarins, *pomarance* (a local sweet orange) and lemons, the three specialities of the firm that makes it. The Balkans and the Middle East are the home of lemonade or sherbet. In Athens, after a visit to the Parthenon, tourists are taken to a kiosk in a park close to Hadrian's Gate to drink a freshly squeezed lemon;

like the lemonade just alluded to, this is an uplifting experience, for the drink is something special. Italy, the country of lemons, does not know how to produce a good bottled lemonade. This is not easy because lemon juice changes flavour the moment it is squeezed from the fruit, and starts to go off – a point that escapes those inept barmen who keep on the counter not a fine basket of lemons but a bottle of the juice squeezed that morning, or even the day before.

(I'm sorry I never saw the Acropolis when it was a Turkish village, hutments knocked together out of bits of the ruins, a mosque inside the Parthenon, a second one in the Erechtheum; like the Roman Forum when it was used to graze sheep.)

Sliced Chicory

There was a time when people ate and drank more (more, that is, if they could, less if they couldn't). I'm not talking of Homeric banquets, nor of Trimalchio, nor of the meals consumed in inns by the Three Musketeers. According to Brillat-Savarin, described by Paolo Valera as 'the celebrated cook of the Sun King', General Bisson got through eight bottles of wine each day for lunch. As for the worthy Curé de Bregnier, here is Brillat-Savarin again: 'Although it had only just gone midday, I found him already at table. The soup and the boiled beef had been cleared away, and these two compulsory dishes had been followed by a leg of mutton *alla reale* and a very fine capon, and a plentiful salad [. . .] Next a large white cheese was brought, out of which he cut a wedge at an angle of ninety degrees.'

Nowadays the thought of eating a starter, first course, second course, dessert and cheese is beginning to seem excessive to many people. Tommaseo, who is in many ways a modern writer, was modern at table as well. Not that he was all that modest an eater, but it is the choice of dishes that makes him feel so close to us. Here is a list of some of them as noted in his *Diario intimo*:

[Florence, 16 March 1833] Vermicelli, meat, pigeon, chicory.
[17 March] Rice, roast veal, salad, salami: for supper pigeon.
[18 March] Vermicelli, beef, calf's head, calf's liver, baked chicory. For supper, braised beef and apples.
[19 March] Beans, eggs, asparagus: for lunch, apples and grapes. For supper, egg, anchovies and grapes.
[23 March] Dunked bread, beans, dried salt cod, herring, apples.
[4 April] Beans, sole, squid, artichokes, pancakes, apple.
[27 April] Broad beans, braised beef and salad.
[16 May] Runner beans, anchovies, herring, trifle.
[25 December] Noodles, meat, capon, sweets given by Colomba.
[Paris, 25 May 1834] Asparagus, artichoke, sole, egg custard.
[Bastia, 8 March 1839] Lemonades, sublimate, syrup of mercury. Chicken, chicory.

The last meal, at Bastia, sadly reflects in the first part the illness that had overtaken Tommaseo. Luckily it ends with a perfect dish: chicken and chicory. Chicory, unless it is the type from Trieste, needs to be sliced very thinly – there's

MENU July 19 1969

Dinner

Turkish Olives   Prosciuto Besant
        Tomato Salad w. Basil & Onion
        Cucumbers àlla Fino
Scotty's Lobster sauce vinaigrette
        Mixed Salad
Boiled Potatoes à la Gigi

Chocolate Mints   Pound Cake
Ice Cream   Grapes

Tuborg beer   Chilean Riesling   St Emilion
Fine Courvoisier Scotch & Soda   Gin & Tonic

a special knack that transforms it into a soft,
aromatic green cloud. Sliced chicory needs a
soft-boiled egg, which in a restaurant is often
rock-hard and is served already shelled, possibly
with the odd fingerprint on its porcelain-white.
Out on a picnic it may be convenient to grasp an

egg that's not leaking all over the place, but with sliced chicory the egg has to be barely hard-boiled, the yolk still soft and the white only just set. When mixed with the salad, the egg seems almost to disappear, but the chicory comes out incredibly softened, and more digestible. As someone has said: 'To eat is human, to digest divine.'

The original and full title of Brillat-Savarin's work is: *La Physiologie du Goût, ou Méditations de gastronomie transcendante. Ouvrage théorique historique et à l'ordre du jour, dédié aux gastronomes parisiens, par un professeur, membre de plusieurs sociétés savantes.* Now Marie-Antoine (Antonin) Carême, the most eminent French chef (his name translates as Lent), chef to Talleyrand and later to the emperors of Russia and Austria, author of a number of books including the five volumes of *L'Art de la cuisine au dix-neuvième siècle,* passes a severe judgment on Brillat-Savarin (even Baudelaire and others have hauled him over the coals),[1] a judgment that I reproduce from Alexandre Dumas's *Le Grand dictionnaire de cuisine.* 'Neither Cambacérès nor Brillat-Savarin ever knew the first thing about dining. Both of them went in for hearty, plebeian dishes. They merely filled their paunches. That is the truth of the matter. Savarin was a great

[1] See Jean-Paul Aron, *The Art of Eating in France: manners and menus in the nineteenth century,* trans. Nina Rootes, 1975.

trencherman [. . .] At the end of the meal he was absorbed with his digestion. I have seen him asleep.' The fact is, though, that Brillat-Savarin, or brillant Savourain, as James Joyce called him in *Finnegans Wake*, did know how to write.

Carême had started life as a pastry-cook, which was not unusual among talented chefs. When still but a lad he would, after a long day's work, stay up late into the night to study drawing; occasionally, with his master's permission, he would stop in at the Print Collection with a view to study, and to seek inspiration for those marvellous inventions in the pastry-cook's line which were soon to make his reputation, and which still survive in certain wedding cakes. He has said: 'The fine arts number five: painting, sculpture, poetry, music and architecture – whose principal sub-division is the art of the pastry-cook.'

I believe that Talleyrand was capable of inventing dishes even without his cook's help. The *garniture Talleyrand* – a sauce for macaroni that's out of this world, made from butter, cheese (Gruyère and Parmesan), foie gras cut into cubes, and truffles – is a recipe which, for its golden simplicity and at the same time the princely luxury of its ingredients, cannot but have emerged from his brain. In France, truffles are to be found in Périgord, and Talleyrand's name was in fact Talleyrand-Périgord; moreover, in winter he was wont to protect himself from the cold by wearing a black woollen cap with two long ear-muffs that dangled down each side of his face, much like the ears of a truffle hound.

Olla podrida

The writer who never talks about eating, about appetite, hunger, food, about cooks and meals, arouses my suspicion, as though some vital element were missing in him. In the opening lines of his novel Cervantes lets us know just what Don Alonso Quejana, the future Don Quixote, habitually ate over the seven days of the week: for lunch, a 'stew with rather more shin of beef than leg of lamb, the leftovers for supper most nights, lardy eggs on Saturdays, lentil broth on Fridays and an occasional pigeon as a Sunday treat'.[1] In many parts of Spain the *olla* is the mainstay of the midday meal: it is a sort of mixed stew, a *pot-au-feu* with chickpeas. *Olla* means casserole. For our Roman ancestors it was an earthenware pot in which to store the ashes (the memory) of the departed. The simple common-or-garden pot is transformed on feast days into *olla podrida* (French *potpourri*), which literally means putrescent saucepan and, in Spanish culinary terms, a mixture (perhaps somewhat chaotic) of all manner of

[1] *Don Quixote*, trans. John Rutherford, 2000.

26

meats and greens: beef, mutton, pork – trotters, ears and tail – partridge, chicken, raw ham, bacon, sausages and, in addition to the chickpeas, carrots, leeks, onions, cabbage, potatoes, lettuce. It is one of the dishes brought to Sancho Panza's table for his first meal as governor of the island of Barattaria. 'That great big steaming dish . . .', says Sancho, 'looks like *olla podrida* to me, and since that sort of hotch-potch stew has got so many different foodstuffs in it, I can't fail to come across one that I'll like and will do me good.'[2]

Olla podrida is singularly appropriate for Sancho Panza because it does not partake of *haute cuisine* but derives rather from the obsessions of the so-called starvelings who, being unable to eat their fill every day, do want now and then to be able to eat whatever they fancy.

The first and most extraordinary dish of this kind – the making of which is from some standpoints reminiscent of the casting of Benvenuto Cellini's *Perseus* – was served up to the Athenians in 389 BC as the festive conclusion to Aristophanes's comedy *The Ecclesiazusae*, and it may be roughly defined as a stew made with oysters, the larger varieties of fish, lampreys, brains, hot sauce, crushed coconut, cheese, honey, leeks, thrushes, pigeons, including wood pigeon, chickens, mullet, hares, pickles, etc. . . . One translator has even identified, among the ingredients of

[2] *Ibid.*, Book II, Chapter 47.

these colossal *potpourri*, ouzo, the strong Greek aniseed liqueur.

The name of this ancient *olla podrida*, which I transcribe into Latin characters to make it less tiring to read, gives an idea not so much of the goodness of the dish as of the number of ingredients used on the occasion by the cooks of that popular recipe: Lapadotemachoselachogaleokranioleipsanodrimhypotrimmatosilphioparaomelitokatakechymenochichlepikossyphophattoperisteralektryonopteckephalliokigklopeleiolagoiosiraiohaphetraganopterigon.

In the matter of cookbooks and books on cuisine, perhaps the saying of Pliny the Younger carries more weight than it does for anything else: 'There is no book however bad that does not have some good in it.' So many have been written that it is almost impossible to find a title for each of them. The earliest of them, by the Sicilian Archestratus, had practically exhausted them all because, as we are told by Atheneus of Naucratis, its title was, according to Chrysippus, *Gastronomy*; according to Lincaeus and Callimachus, *The Good Table*; according to Clearchus, *The Art of Cooking* and, according to others, *The Kitchen*.

In periods of decadence the cult of the kitchen becomes excessive. Pliny complained that a cook cost more than a horse. 'Clito', wrote La Bruyère in *The Characters*, 'had but two occupations in life: to eat lunch in the morning and supper in the evening.'

By contrast it is a pleasure to read the reply given by John Updike to a woman interviewing him, who asked him what had been his most memorable meal: 'My most memorable meal was a lunch with Alfred Knopf [the eminent publisher], who took me to La Côte Basque [the famous New York restaurant] when it was still owned by Henri Soulé [the distinguished French chef]. I can't remember what we ate but . . .'[3]

[3] Mimi Sheraton, 'John Updike Ruminates on Matters Gustatory', New York Times, 15 December 1982.

Spaghetti Bolognese, Overcooked

When I was small, gold teeth, glasses and a paunch seemed to me signs of importance, even of beauty. Where grown-ups had a tummy, all I had was a hole, to symbolise the fact that I didn't count: I had no weight, no authority.

At one o'clock the first bathers started to make for the *pensione*. The man with the paunch, the gold teeth and the glasses summoned the beach attendant with a gesture and had a plate of pasta brought to him, right there as he sat in his chair at the water's edge. A large plate. With tomato sauce. And plenty of cheese.

Possibly the spaghetti served on the beach by the attendant was not *al dente*. But never mind, given how famished one was after a swim. I followed, boggle-eyed, every forkful, each one neatly rolled up, as it travelled from the plate to the gold teeth; I savoured the taste of the tomato just as if it had been in my own mouth . . .

Then came the age of understanding (of spaghetti *al dente*) and finally the age of crisis.

Now and then I am overcome by a violent yearning for canteen cookery (be it school, barracks, office, hospital), for a plate of 'back-to-front' pasta.

I dash into the nearest trattoria, sit down, and without even looking at the menu order a plate of spaghetti Bolognese. I don't ask for it to be cooked to order, so I'm letting myself in for an overcooked portion; and I ask for Bolognese sauce, which I normally consider the very one to be avoided, because at that juncture it is precisely the sauce I want. I even want to shout to the waiter: 'And take care it comes on a cold plate!' but there is no need, the plate will be icy.

Once I've devoured the overcooked spaghetti in its nondescript sauce – with pleasure, may I add – the crisis is over. For a good while I shall revert to asking for spaghetti cooked to order, *al dente*, and make a fuss if that's not what I get.

There is something in this story that is reminiscent of the strange case of Dr Jekyll and Mr Hyde. If a friend (Dr Lanyon) were to come into the trattoria and catch me gorging myself on overcooked spaghetti in a 'Bolognese' sauce, the analogy would be stronger still.

Augustus's Asparagus

Suetonius is the favourite reading of the chef Allen Lieb who enjoyed a moment of celebrity in the United States in 1979, thanks to (or blame it on) the writer John McPhee, a great fan of his, who had written an extensive profile of him in the *New Yorker*, while guarding, as Lieb wished, the secret of his real name and the name and location of his restaurant (a secret which could not, however, hold out for long against the unbridled stampede of the press).

Lieb is an interesting cook, not so much for his professional bravura as for the way he works and the way he speaks about his calling: he has not the smallest desire for publicity, prefers using his hands rather than implements, likes leftovers, does not throw away spent matches, never cooks a dish the same way twice, claims that the most important thing to learn is to take one's time. His conversation, as Monselet would say, is nourishing.

At night, before turning in after a hard day, Allen Lieb reads *The Lives of the Twelve Caesars*: emperors greedy for food and drink, for sumptuous meals, strange and highly extravagant dishes, unheard-of cruelties. Tiberius, Caligula, Claudius, Nero, Galba, Vitellius and Domitian all met a violent end, their throats cut, or strangled or poisoned. Claudius, a glutton for *Amanita cesarea* mushrooms, was killed during a banquet by one of these choice delicacies cooked in poison. Vitellius, whose gluttony had surprised the world – here in Italy the name alone has a familiar ring in the kitchen – tried shortly before he was assassinated and thrown into the Tiber to escape in a litter, 'taking with him only his cook and his baker'.

Not even 'the goodly Augustus', to quote Dante, was that model of perfection he is generally held to be thanks to one's schooling. Falsely suspecting the Praetor Quintus Gallus of treachery, 'he had his centurions and soldiers lay hold of him and cruelly torture him as though he had been a slave; and as he would not confess, he first plucked out his eyes with his own hand, then had him put to death'. 'Attalus, his chancellor, had his legs broken because he had shown someone a letter of his in exchange for fifty crowns.' And 'being inflamed with lust for a gentlewoman at a banquet, her husband having been a consul and attending the banquet with her, he rose from the table and, in her husband's presence, led her off into a bedroom, after which he brought her back to the table, her ears still red and her hair dishevelled'.

He didn't even have the build of a great man: 'small of stature' and 'teeth few, small and riddled with tartar'. He was 'a weedy little runt'. But he did not scant the kitchen because 'when he wanted to express the speed of something done in haste, he would say: "Faster than it takes to cook asparagus".' The sixteenth-century Italian translation of Suetonius's book (by Brother Paolo del Rosso) is a joy, except for the commas, which seem to be put in at random, 'hither and yon, catch as catch can, like capers in tartare sauce', as Gadda would say.

In Rome there is no longer anything august in the name Augustus. It's a barman's name: 'Augusto, a coffee!'

The True Cook

The sculptor Arturo Martini had a most impoverished childhood. He had five years' schooling: two years in the first form and three in the second. He was the son of a cook, and on the subject of cooking he made a very pertinent observation, as recorded by Gino Scarpa in his conversations with the sculptor: 'Cooking is a matter of instinct. Others might need to taste the soup, I can tell at a glance if it is salted. There is the Artusi,[1] and beyond him, there's the unreachable.' That's how it is. The true cook does not taste, it's a little like the pianist who plays without looking at the keyboard.

[1] Pellegrino Artusi is the author of the most famous Italian cookbook.

Egg on Leeks

'Mixed salad *antipasto*: groundnuts in Apicius's dressing – oil and wine.'[1] Thus begins a recipe in Apicius's *De re coquinaria*, the bestselling work of gastronomy in antiquity, destined to last, with however many revisions, cuts, insertions, repunctuations, longer than the Roman Forum. Here you will find recipes, not all that easy to interpret, for the most celebrated dishes from ancient Roman cuisine: baked sows' udders, roast crane in honey sauce, parrots' tongues . . . but above all, note the excessive presence among the recipes of a sauce that the translator calls 'Apicius's dressing' while the author uses an ugly word, *liquamen*. This sauce is something of a gastronomic mystery: nobody has ever been able to explain precisely what it is. The introduction talks of an 'ingredient [. . .] based on herbs, spices, vinegar and, possibly, fish paste'. Apicius does not give the recipe, for in his day it needed no description;

[1] *De re coquinaria*, trans. as Apicius, *Cookery and Dining in Imperial Rome*, by Joseph Dommers Vehling, 1977. See also *The Roman Cookery of Apicius*, trans. John Edwards, 1988.

he gives instructions only for altering the flavour of the *liquamen*, if it has acquired a nasty taste, with the aid of smoke from laurel and cypress. The best *liquamen*, according to an advertisement discovered on a wall in Pompeii, was the percolation obtained from the firm of Umbricus Agathopus.

Some time ago a friend showed me a tiny bottle of Nuoc-Mam, a sauce widely used in Vietnam, and when he told me it was made with salt, spices, herbs and fish left to putrefy in the sun, I gathered that Nuoc-Mam could not be anything other than the mysterious sauce of Apicius. According to my friend, who had sampled it, the said sauce was 'OK for Vietnamese'.

'Once they are cooked,' continues Apicius, who probably dictated his complicated recipes in a very deep, cavernous voice characteristic of Romans of every epoch, 'put in to boil with them some pork liver, chicken livers, trotters and small birds cut up. Once they come to the boil, crush and add some pepper and ligustico.[2] Steep in *liquamen*, wine and raisin liqueur in order to sweeten it. Pour on some of the juice itself: and turn it out on to the groundnuts. Once it has boiled, add starch immediately to thicken it.'

Enough to cut the appetite. Or rather, what is required, in contrast, is simpler fare: Horace's leeks and chickpeas, Bertoldo's turnips and beans

[2] A medicinal plant found chiefly in Liguria. (Translator)

37

and, I should like to add, those eggs on leeks proposed by Schino (Franceschino).

Boil the leeks (the poor man's asparagus), drain them, put two or three (only a few, otherwise they drown the flavour of the eggs) warm on to a hot plate, chop them up small and slip over them an egg fried in plenty of frothy butter. The butter mingles with the remaining water from the leeks to make a delectable little sauce. Should be accompanied by a good glass of Clinto or Bonarda (a light Lombard red).

And the wine, let it be cool! This taste for red wine drunk chilled, which many would-be connoisseurs frown upon, is, I am happy to see, endorsed by Bocuse: 'I serve wines well chilled; particularly Beaujolais. I serve Burgundy at 10–12°C, white wines at 8–10°, Bordeaux at 15–16°. Many people think that to "*chambrer*" a wine means placing it in the hearth or by the boiler; actually what it means is putting it in an unheated room!'[3] Why this title, *La Cuisine du marché*? Because Bocuse rightly says that instead of deciding on a menu and then going to the market to buy the ingredients, what is needed is to do as he does for his famous restaurant outside Lyons: go first to the market and then decide on the menu in the light of the best and most suitable items on offer. For the same reason he advises against

[3] Paul Bocuse, *La Cuisine du marché* (*The New Cuisine*, trans. Colette Rossant and Lorraine Davis, 1978).

buying new-crop fruit and vegetables. One can only agree with him.

But faced, in the cuisine and the cookbook of 'Lyons's gastronomical comet', with a measure of excess in refinement and luxury, even in the way a dish is set out on the plate, it is impossible entirely to blame Alexander Cockburn, writing a review in the 8 December 1977 issue of the *New York Review of Books*, where he defined Bocuse's labours as 'a costly exercise in gastro-porn'.

After the recipes of Apicius I can even (for a moment!) understand those who take not the slightest interest in eating and drinking. Among them must be numbered the writer Lucio Mastronardi, the master (or Master) of Vigevano.

'Mastronardi, do you enjoy your food?'

'Couldn't care less.'

'But do you have some favourite dish?'

'Leaving aside liver, brains and tripe, I eat anything.'

'Do you drink wine with your meal?'

'No, mineral water.'

'Why?'

'Because that's what my wife buys.'

Sculpted Meat

The restaurant was all in aluminium: walls, ceiling, floor, tables. The plates were aluminium discs. The guests were enjoying themselves. The sculpted meat (in French, *viande sculptée*), the most famous dish in futuristic cuisine, was the focus of general curiosity. According to the definition (recipe) of Fillia, who invented it, this is 'made from a large cylindrical meatball concocted from roast veal, and stuffed with eleven different kinds of cooked vegetable. This cylinder, placed vertically on the centre of the dish, is crowned with a thick coating of honey, and supported at the base by a sausage ring that rests [somewhat like certain Roman obelisks] on three golden balls of chicken meat'.[1] Sculpted meat (like FIAT chicken and so many other dishes that energised futurist meals), has loomed in the gastronomic heavens like a meteor that gleams for a few seconds and suddenly vanishes, leaving not a trace. Today, we would consider it not so much a dish of the future as

[1] This, like the other excerpts quoted, is from F. T. Marinetti and Fillia, *La cucina futurista*, 1932; reissued in English as *The Futurist Cookbook*, 1989.

some recipe out of Apicius, some leftover of Trimalchio's, something old-hat. 'If there is one art that is recalcitrant to futurism,' Olindo Guerrini has wisely written, 'it is the culinary art.'

The futurists, however, had no hesitation.

'What of the old cuisine?' Fillia was asked. 'What will survive?'

'Not a thing, barely the old pots and pans.'

Probably the real aim of the authors of futuristic recipes was to write something worthwhile, and their mistake was in their wish to pass from the printed page to the fully realised dish: '. . . it would be a question of reading the book [*The Futurist Cookbook*], not only in the context of futuristic "behaviourism", but also in the light of Lévi-Strauss's *The Raw and the Cooked*. Apart from the fact that those recipes are, above all, poetry. As for the practical side, I shall ask my wife to cook a couple of them, if only to see whether they add up to anything in gastronomic terms.'[2]

No, in my view they simply don't add up. They are merely for reading. Besides, what is that hideous war memorial in Como if it is not a 'recipe' realised by, of all people, the futurist architect Sant'Elia? (Whose plans prefigured not so much the future *ville radieuse*, ever lying ahead, as the impending horrors of modern-day building.)

In May 1930 Marinetti went to meet his friends Prampolini and Fillia in a villa on Lake Trasimeno; the plan was to collaborate on a special exhibition meal in order to avert a lover's suicide. Gone midnight, the exhibition of edible sculpture was ready. The lady they were expecting arrived. But . . .

'A long, silent pause knocked out Marinetti, Prampolini and Fillia. The lady stared at them for a few minutes, then keeled over backwards and fell asleep herself. The feeble flutter of their breathing laden with desires, imaginings and impulses blended with the gurgle and rustle of the reed-bed in the Lake as it was riffled by the evening breeze.'

Do we want to interpret this sleep? Or confine ourselves to recording that Gabriele d'Annunzio, who happened to be passing through, was heard to mutter: 'I possess that which I have imparted.'

[2] From a letter of Glauco Viazzi.

Farfalle alla matriciana

A cold mist hung over Vicolo Capre, Via Rugabella, Via Velasca. It was striking noon.

What about lunch? . . . Where? . . . What kind? . . .

Eternal problem.

I thought of the trattoria hollowed out of the side of the red church of San Nazaro, where I had dined a few evenings earlier with a friend: Lilliputian tables, a good woman dressed in light blue, carrying plates of *bucatini alla matriciana*: too red . . . Right after the war I had fetched up one day at Amatrice, in the Sabine hills, and had stopped there for a meal, and almost certainly I must have eaten *bucatini alla matriciana*; but, in my ignorance of matters culinary, I paid no attention either to the *bucatini* or to Amatrice, and thus I'm left with no recollection of the meal, important though it was from a certain angle. I see someone putting his hand up, he wants to make an observation.

I know already what he is going to say. 'You should be saying *all'amatriciana*, from Amatrice, not *alla matriciana*.'

This is true: cultivated people say *all'amatriciana*. Uncultivated people, however, say *alla matriciana*, and the preferences of the uncultured carry, as is well known, a great weight in questions of linguistic usage. Moreover there is the natural tendency for every derivative word to acquire its own distinct, autonomous form, departing as far as possible from its matrix (the *amatriciana* tendency). . . .

Later I was to discover just how exquisite *bucatini alla matriciana* can be, how light and delicate they are, even if the sauce does include bacon, oil and onion; thanks also to the small peppers. Carnacina quite rightly states that the bacon is to be cut into pieces that are not too small, and to go rather easy on the tomato. The pasta ought to be pink rather than bright red. The bacon should come to about one quarter of the weight of the pasta.

Avezzano was the base from which I had advanced as far as Amatrice with a small company looking out for film locations. After supper our local colleagues joined us at the restaurant.

'Have you eaten?'

'Yes, yes. We've had supper.'

'What will you have?'

'Nothing, thank you . . .'

The faces, however, did not suggest a decided negative.

'A dessert? . . . A coffee? . . .'

There was a moment of embarrassed silence, during which the men exchanged a few glances in the Abruzzi dialect. Then the leader said: 'All right, if you insist . . . we'll have a *bucatino alla matriciana.*'

The waiter, who was passing by with two bowls brimful of soup (his coarse thumbs, their nails rimmed with indelible black, were constantly dipping into the broth), was perilously brought to a stop; the order was passed to him by many voices, and as he went on his way he was struck in the back with a final injunction: 'And don't stint on that *bucatino*!'

The custom of filling soup bowls to the brim still obtains in many unpretentious eating places where often, however, the fare is by no means to be dismissed. A soup thus served may be defined as 'a soup on the nail'. (Were the bowl not so full, the customer would be entitled to protest that his helping was too meagre.) These are the places where, at the bar, the glasses of wine, white or red, are equally filled to the brim, indeed beyond the brim so that the wine protrudes without overflowing, however, thanks to the physical phenomenon known as the surface tension of liquids. As dextrous as the barman, the customer carries the glass to his lips without any spillage; and as a rule he drains it at a single draught, acquiring the right to emit at the end a loud liberating sigh.

I cross Piazza San Nazaro, turn into Vicolo Santa Caterina, closed off to traffic by three granite bollards, and enter the trattoria. My friend is at his usual table, sitting in front of (or more precisely, notes Wolfgang Hildesheimer, behind) a tankard of beer and a plate of *bucatini alla matriciana*.

'*Bucatini* for me too! And make that a special order!'

While I give my order to the waitress in light blue who is heading for the kitchen with a pile of dirty dishes, I manage to catch her eye. I know from experience that orders given to a waiter on the run are only fulfilled if one manages to look him in the eye. Then, like a wild beast mortally wounded, he takes refuge in his lair (the kitchen) and passes the order. Almost at once, in fact (too fast to be a special order), the *bucatini* are placed in front of me.

Bucatini are a miracle even from a technical angle. It is hard to understand how a machine can spew out spaghetti *with a hole through the middle*. This is not, however, the moment to be losing oneself in problems of too great substance. I mix and roll up the first forkful. I think of foreigners, for whom to roll up a forkful of spaghetti is a well-nigh impossible task and yet who for centuries have persisted in ordering spaghetti. Can one be more backward in cooking? Why, let them order *penne alla matriciana*! *Rigatoni, farfalle alla matriciana*![1]

---

[1] All pasta shapes that may be speared with a fork rather than rolled round the prongs. (Translator)

Besides, *bucatini* have to be as slippery as eels – a person will easily finish up with his sauce on the tablecloth, or on his shirt, or on his tie, or his trousers, or on the carpet. But no authentic pasta eater will allow the joy of the moment to be spoiled by these inevitable accidents. No talcum powder – its scent would ruin everything. We'll put it on later. The ideal would be to spool up the *bucatini* while sitting comfortably, bare-chested, in the shade of a pinewood, followed with alert eyes by the faithful hound which, as is well known, relishes the taste of the *bucatini* a great deal more than his master does, for a dog's sense of smell is exactly a million times more sensitive than a human's.

One-egg Omelette

The egg is today the least expensive thing to eat. Should you want to know an egg's degree of freshness, the vendor would point out to you three signs: 'Fresh', 'Very fresh', 'For drinking' – from which you conclude that those marked fresh are the least fresh.

The moment you mention eggs a thousand problems arise. Which are better? Those with white shells or those with brown? The large or the small ones? Those with a yellow yolk or those with an orange one?

The fried egg is given as an example of basic cookery, so basic that the cookbooks tend to make no mention of it. But it too has its secrets. You cook it on a low heat; you don't put it into the pan directly from its shell but from a cup: only the white to begin with, holding the yolk back with a spoon; then, when the white starts to set, you sprinkle it with salt and pepper and pour the yolk on top of it, right in the middle, and thus avoid too direct and searing a contact with the bottom of the pan. The cooking is completed with the lid on the pan; that way the egg cooks (just a little) on its upper side. Once it's ready you transfer it on to a warm plate to avoid it over-cooking in the heat of the pan. It is possible to add a little of the olive oil or butter (frothy) in which it was cooked. But if the egg is being cooked with bacon it has to be picked up with a spatula so that whatever it is cooked in drains off, and it is placed dry on the warm plate.

If there is more to frying an egg than meets the eye, imagine what is involved in an omelette. Raymond Oliver, proprietor of the old Paris restaurant Au Grand Véfour, which was Colette's restaurant of choice: 'A work of art is always an adventure: the omelette does not escape this rule.'[1]

Myself, I also like omelettes the way they do them in Germany: with just one egg (plus flour and milk). Here is the recipe.

In a bowl mix well two spoonfuls of flour and about a teacup of milk.[2] The resulting batter should be fairly liquid and smooth. Add salt, then a beaten egg, and continue mixing. Pour the mixture into a non-stick pan in which you have heated up some oil and butter. As soon as the mixture sets, flip the omelette over, adding a knob of butter. Reduce the heat, cover and cook for at

[1] Among dishes served at the Grand Véfour are L'Œuf au Plat Louis Oliver (Raymond's father).
[2] On the vexed question of exact measurements used in recipes, see what the author says under 'How to Write Out a Recipe' on p. 142. (Translator)

least another five minutes, giving the pan a shake every now and then to prevent catching. If the pan is on the small side, your batter is enough for two omelettes.

What goes well with an omelette is lettuce in a German dressing, with soured cream (yoghurt will do as a substitute), finely chopped onion, vinegar, black pepper and salt. (You can dress cucumber the same way.)

Or you may eat the omelette as a dessert, at the end of a meal, with forest-fruit jam: blackberry, bilberry, bramble.

Needless to say, the fresher the eggs the better the omelette. Bartolomeo Scappi, however, Pope Pius V's personal chef, thought otherwise: 'Take eight two-day-old eggs and whisk them, as these are better for omelettes than fresh ones are, because the fresh ones make them tough and they don't turn out as yellow as the others.'[3]

Is that so? It would seem an excessive refinement, not unlike the one mentioned by Brillat-Savarin: 'Do we not find in our own day those who have discovered the particular flavour of the thigh on which the partridge rests while sleeping?'

Or like that other one from certain oenologists

---

[3] *Opera di Bartolomeo Scappi, mastro dell'arte del cucinare, con la quale si può ammaestrare qualsivoglia Cuoco, Scalco, Trinciante o Mastro di Casa. Divisa in sei libri . . . Con le figure che fanno di bisogno nella Cucina . . .*, Alessandro de' Vecchi, Venice, 1622.

of exceptional refinement, who advise those needing to fetch a good bottle up from the cellar to carry it up extremely slowly, that is, leaving the bottle to stand on each successive step for a day and a night, so as not to traumatise the contents with too rapid a change of temperature.

Rabbit and Polenta

Around Sunday noon from the windows on Via Cavour there issues a savoury smell of rabbit braised in wine. Rabbit sauce is just the thing for polenta. 'It goes down like a letter in the postbox,' Brillat-Savarin observes.

The solitary wayfarer cannot but stop beneath a window, as if from within the kitchen-dining room, threading its way through the geraniums, there came the sound of a most beautiful piece of music to fill his lungs greedily. However, the Sunday silence reigns supreme, to the point of making one think that the rabbit, giving final evidence of his inbred good nature, is attending to his own cooking.

But this is not the case. Rather, the first labour to be effected is not all that straightforward: take a rabbit weighing one and a half kilos and chop it up small, taking care not to splinter the bones.

Stop for a breather – have a sip of white wine, good and chilled, and return to your rabbit. Brown the pieces in oil and butter, with rosemary and black pepper. Salt them, then add a glass of white wine and reduce this by half. Pour on enough stock to cover the (now unrecognisable) rabbit: this, according to Chinese cooks, is all to the good, whereas the ancient Romans, after cooking a pheasant or a peacock (whole), did their best to carry to the table a pheasant or peacock that looked as close as could be to the living bird, sticking back in the feathers plucked out before cooking and getting it to assume as natural a position as possible on the serving dish.

Cover the rabbit and cook on a low heat. It will need to simmer for about an hour and a half. After three-quarters of an hour you may add the odd vegetable (but go easy): diced potatoes, peas, fresh beans. Then prepare the following complement to the sauce, to be added a quarter of an hour before the end of the cooking time, with a little chopped parsley: put a knob of butter and a spoonful of flour into a cup and pour on some of the boiling stock, a little at a time, constantly stirring it in with the wooden spoon. Then pour this into the pan with the rabbit and mix well. The sauce, which is the best thing about the dish, has to be plentiful and not too thick. Meanwhile someone will have prepared the polenta.

In Via Cavour, above the entrance to the house where I spend the summer, a modest fresco depicts St Lawrence bearing in front of him, upright, the instrument of his martyrdom: the gridiron. Whereof, quite unintentionally, the saint indicates the best use (in the kitchen): standing upright, in front of the fire, not laid over it. In this way, the fat melted by the heat does not drip on to the hot coals, encouraging a smoky flame that, without waiting for embers to form, gives a nasty taste of snuffed-out candle to the food; moreover, it is even possible to cook so long as the wood has caught. To hold a sandwich-style gridiron – one to clamp a steak, say – all that is needed is to rest it against the larger four-footed grill which normally is laid on the hot coals but here is to be placed against the fire pushed to the back of the stove.

For chicken it is ideal. Cut the bird into quarters and clamp the pieces in the gridiron, keeping the skin-sides, the more fatty parts, all together and facing downwards, where the heat will be greater. Salt the chicken, grind on a generous amount of black pepper, add a few bay and sage leaves and sprigs of rosemary. Clamp the gridiron shut and place the skin-side, the fattier side, in front of and close to the fire first of all, grilling it until it is well done. Don't be afraid of overdoing it: all the fat needs to drip away, leaving the skin crisp, dark, almost seared. Turn the pieces over. In the absence of the fat from the skin, scorch them somewhat less. Then move the gridiron back from the heat so as to cook the inside of the pieces more slowly. About another half hour and the chicken is cooked.

For a touch of refinement, keep handy a small bunch of wild fennel or bay leaves, to set alight on the hot coals at the last moment and pass the chicken over them, without overdoing the process. Anyone who has tried meat cooked this way does what the Indian tiger used to do after it had tasted human flesh – it would no longer touch anything else.

Stuffed Pigeon

The Grotte del Piccione, in Via della Vite, in Rome, is a restaurant that originated in 1927 in a cave owned by the grandfather of the present proprietors on his estate at Pineta Sacchetti; here he would invite his friends to come and dine *al fresco*. Above the cave there were some dovecotes. In 1930 the Grotto dei Piccioni, as the poet Trilussa had christened it, moved to Via della Vite (this being more accessible). It is no longer a cave, and above it, instead of pigeons, there are the building's residents. But perhaps the odd pigeon has remained, on the restaurant menu. . . . The word restaurant cannot help reminding me of a character out of the writer Antonio Delfini, seated (more or less) at table: 'It was ten at night: facing me, seated at a table by the kitchen door, were five characters, one of whom (not sitting down but crouching like a dog) was a large hunting dog.'

Pigeons fall into two categories: the edible and the inedible. The inedible type is taking over Milan. A first group (who on earth installed them?) proliferates in the Piazza del Duomo.

Hence colonies of wayfarer pigeons fan out in all directions, fleeing the tourists, the standardised pigeon feed and the photographers. If in place of the inedible pigeons there were chickens, they . . . would not be there. And the Piazza del Duomo would not be the same. Instead of which our pigeons increase and multiply quite alarmingly.

Lieutenant F. Hall 'observed a flock of pigeons betwixt Frankfurt and the Indiana territory, one mile at least in breadth; it took up four hours in passing; which, at the rate of one mile per minute, gives a length of 240 miles; and, supposing three pigeons to each square yard, gives 2,230,272,000 pigeons.'[1] Enough to feed India and China with a single flock.

The tribe of North American wayfarer pigeons is, however, extinct. The final specimen, a female known as Martha, died on 1 September 1914 in Cincinnati Zoo, probably without realising that she was the last of so many millions of brothers and sisters. Her embalmed body may be viewed in the Smithsonian Institution, Washington, DC.

We are so used to considering pigeons as pests, inedible fowl like swallows and rooks, that when we meet them on a restaurant menu we are as surprised as if we had read: stuffed crow, or crow with olives, or crow *à la mode*. In fact pigeons – the good ones – have always been eaten and enjoyed. Dovecotes were, once upon a time, to be found all over the place, often beautifully designed, like the one at Minerbio ascribed to Vignola. In the Veneto those pigeons that roost in the towers are considered an extra-special delicacy. To have them always available, restaurateurs preserve them in barrels, like anchovies, ready to appear promptly on the table.

[1] See 'The Thousand and Second Tale of Scheherazade', in *Tales of Mystery and Imagination* by Edgar Allan Poe.

What is the best season for pigeon? Well, for pigeons it is always the right season (albeit, from their viewpoint, the wrong season). They hatch every two months and may be eaten at twenty-five days.

And the best way to cook them? We cannot do better than mention Gadda's stuffed pigeons, 'roasted in a casserole with sprigs of rosemary and new potatoes, moderately sweet and on the small side, a touch overcooked but seasoned by the gravy produced by these very pigeons, which are themselves stuffed, in their turn, according to an Andalusian recipe, with oregano, sage, basil, thyme, rosemary, wild mint, peppers, raisins, lard, chicken brains, ginger, paprika, cloves and additional potatoes, as though the ones serving as accompaniment, that is, placed outside the pigeon's rump, were not sufficient – those ones would have reverted to pigeon flesh, as it were, a second time, so much had they been assimilated: just as if the bird, once roasted, had acquired innards more in keeping with its new status as roast chicken, but smaller and plumper than a chicken because it was, after all, a pigeon.'[2]
Which brings us back to Delfini.

---

[2] Carlo Emilio Gadda, *Acquainted with Grief*. There is an English translation by William Weaver, 1969. The strange thing is that Gadda, who displayed such zeal in describing gastronomical wonders and was himself no mean trencherman, found the business of cooking an unbearable torture.

Which wine, then? Forget about the wine waiter, and let us stick with Gadda: 'A five-year-old white extra dry, now, from Cavalier Gabbioni Empedocle & Figlio, Albano Laziale, something to dream about even in a police cell, the wine, the glass, the Father, Son, and Lazio.'[3]

Gadda is author of a notable recipe for risotto alla Milanese, 'Risotto patrio. Rècipe',[4] which has lately been analysed and compared with the corresponding recipe from Artusi, in a study undertaken by the Italian Seminar at the University of Fribourg (Switzerland), published by Juris Verlag, Zürich, 1975. 'The preparation of the risotto is not prescribed, it is narrated'; therein lies the fundamental difference.

Not, alas, that the good recipe suffices by itself; the flavour of risotto alla Milanese is somewhat less palatable because the saffron, which gives it that extraordinary flavour, emerges more insipid year by year from its little envelope. Saffron from Aquila, this unrecognised Italian treasure, is ever harder to find and is being replaced by imported saffron that is almost tasteless and reduced to a mere colouring agent.

What may be eaten with risotto alla Milanese – and this may cause surprise to some – are pickled onions. Here's how.

With your spoon (the true Milanese eats risotto

[3] Carlo Emilio Gadda, *That Awful Mess on the Via Merulana*. There is also an English translation of this by William Weaver, 1985.
[4] Carlo Emilio Gadda, *Le Meraviglie d'Italia*, Einaudi, Turin, 1964. The amount of saffron in the recipe is possibly excessive: two coffeespoons for eight people; further reduced, 'for scrupulous stomachs', to two level coffeespoonfuls.

with a spoon because it is cooked very moist, though it may perfectly well be eaten with a fork) spread the risotto out well on the plate, an operation that strikes some people as common, like that of tying one's napkin round the back of one's neck, but that is the way it's done anyhow. Scatter round the edge of the risotto, but without invading the edge of the plate itself, which must remain spotless, a few small Como onions pickled in red-wine vinegar – and cut into quarters – and sprinkle the risotto with a few drops of the onion-steeped vinegar. Eat the risotto, adding now and then a nibble of the onion.

Finanziera

Via Fiori Chiari, Via San Carpoforo, Via Madonnina . . . beautiful names though somewhat compromised by the recollection of their not-too-distant past as the Red-Light District of Milan. Number 1 Via Madonnina is now closed, its windows boarded up as happens with empty buildings awaiting demolition. It's a decrepit sliver of a building between Via Madonnina and Via Mercato, like so many in the Paris of Utrillo. Here, in Paolo Valera's day, there flourished the most famous of Milan's 300 *'boìs'*, restaurants of the worst sort that the locals called *sesmilaquindes*, in other words 6015: the number of a prisoner in the Bassa, Mantua's jail, and which resembles the word *'boìs'* when written down.

What sort of fare was to be had in a 6015?

Well, a Roma (or *rosticianna*, the worst cuts of meat with onions fried in lard), a Venezia (tripe), a Spaniard (roast potatoes), *màccheri al sughillo* (macaroni in a sauce), *vermi* (worms or *vermicelli*), *nervosi* (*nervetti*, a dish of brawn cut up with pickled vegetables), *galba* (soup), *polenta vedova* (alternate layers of polenta and sauce, or cheese or leftovers, baked in the oven), *el scagliùs* (the scalies: fish), *i trifol* (potatoes), and salad. To end with: a noggin of *rabbiosa* (firewater).

'Soup with three-quarters of mixed bread and *vott* [eight cents' worth] of *bagniffa* [sauce for dunking],' says one customer.

'Fifteen cents' worth of *trotto* [horsemeat],' says another.

'Any wine?'

'Upset tum. Make it a glass of water.'

Waiter (another order): 'Ten cents' worth of *merlo* [cod] for that gentleman at the back . . . *a pée biott* [the one with bare feet].'

To rinse out our mouths let us listen to 'Fricassé, from the Rocher de Cancale', who proposes 'Muriton of red tongue; cauliflowers with *velouté* sauce; veal *à la Sainte-Menehould; marinade à la Sainte-Florentin*; and orange jellies *en mosaïques*.'[1] Fricassé is a character (evidently a gastronome) invented by Poe; the Rocher de Cancale, one of the most famous Paris restaurants in the nineteenth century. As for veal *à la Sainte-Menehould*, Poe gives his explanation in another story: 'A small calf, roasted whole and crouched on its knees on the serving dish, with an apple in its mouth, the way in England they serve hare'.[2]

Sainte-Menehould is a town on the Aisne, the gastronomic capital of Champagne, noted for

[1] Edgar Allan Poe, 'Lionising', *op. cit.*
[2] Edgar Allan Poe, 'The System of Dr Tarr and Professor Fether', *ibid.*

various culinary specialities including the celebrated pig's trotters *à la Sainte-Menehould*.
Alexandre Dumas, in his *Grand dictionnaire de
cuisine*, relates how Desmoulins spread the slander
that Louis XVI was arrested at Sainte-Menehould
(whereas we know he was arrested at Varennes)
because he refused to pass that way without stop-
ping to sample the famous trotters.

Let us go back a step.

'Talk to me about the Marquis de Nointel.'

'Louis de Béchameil, Marquis de Nointel, was
an eminent financier . . . comptroller to the Duke
of Orleans.'

'Very good.'

'He was born in sixteen thirty and died in Paris
in the year one thousand . . .'

'. . . one thousand . . .'

'. . . seven hundred . . .'

'. . . seven hundred . . .'

'. . . and three.'

'Excellent. And what in particular did he
achieve, that his reputation should have survived
to our own day?'

'Well . . . I can't remember . . .'

'Come on! An invention which, wherever it
crops up, carries with it, so to say, a touch of
aristocratic refinement.'

'I don't . . .'

'Which has nothing to do with finance . . . nor
with *la finanziera*, that delicious bridge between
peasant cookery and *haute cuisine* . . . I'll tell you:

Béchameil . . .: Béchamel! Sauce Béchamel, the queen of all white sauces! The sauce mentioned by Pellegrino Artusi as *balsamella* in his book on the art of eating well, for all the world as if it had been invented by Giuseppe Balsamo, who went by the name of Alessandro, Count Cagliostro or indeed Marquis Pellegrino . . .'

But what was I talking about? Oh yes, about *la finanziera*. A highly fantastical dish (or a sauce). Just look at its ingredients: sweetbreads, beef and veal marrow, meatballs, hens' crests, olives, lemon, butter, vinegar, stock, parsley . . . Indeed, the kitchen is undoubtedly the place where the most unlikely couplings take place. Think of the squid

and peas which (as Achille Campanile explains),
'starting, the one from the ocean depths, the
other from the bowels of the earth, meet up in
a frying pan. From here on their destinies are
linked. To begin with there's a certain froideur'
but then, with the aid of the cooking stove . . .

Galen's White Soup

James Fenimore Cooper, in addition to writing *The Last of the Mohicans* and so many other novels well known in their day, was founder and president of The Bread & Cheese Club in New York. The Bread & Cheese Club was also known as the Lunch Club, because 'bread and cheese' was synonymous with lunch, the Anglo-Saxon's light midday meal (as also that of the ancient Greeks and Romans). And in the sixteenth century Gerolamo Cardano was writing in his autobiography: 'At lunch I have always eaten more lightly than at supper.'

His lunch would often consist of a Galen's white soup, that is, chopped leeks boiled in a little water and seasoned with oil, vinegar and salt, and, I should add today, black pepper: an excellent dish, to which Galen certainly ascribed healing properties.

I believe that the white soup was so called because only the white of the leeks was to be used, as any cookbook will tell you; even if often, as we look over the hapless leeks, we lack the courage to follow the advice all the way but toss into the pan a bit of the green part as well, which does not leave the soup tasting any the worse.

Cardano was the most famous physician in Europe during the sixteenth century, and, as a mathematician, showed himself quite capable of illustrating, complete with demonstrations, the solution to cubic equations which Niccolò Tartaglia had arrived at on 2 February 1531. In his autobiography, however, he also mentioned having seen a rooster that spoke to him with a human voice, and, in the matter of cookery, he wrote: 'There are fifteen items requisite in the preparation of food: fire, embers, basin, water, saucepan, frying pan, spit, gridiron, pestle, edge and flat of the knife, grater, parsley, rosemary and bay.' Lombroso thought he was mad.

Graveyard Stew

Springs is a pleasant spot on the coast, not far from New York, with large woods in which you may, as in the days of Fenimore Cooper, come upon deer, wild rabbits, tortoises, foxes, squirrels and black-eyed bears which go rooting about in the dustbins by night.

The last whale was caught in its waters in 1907: it was 57 feet long and produced 2,000 gallons of oil. The last redskins in the area, the Shinnecock, having now abandoned the pages of Cooper's novels, put on folk-dance displays in the summer. The Mohicans, on the other hand, have quite vanished from the face of the earth. The last of the Mohicans, as Cooper relates, was called Uncas (Nimble Deer) and died a hero's death. Thanks to Cooper we are also acquainted with the penultimate of the Mohicans, whose name was Chingachgook (Great Snake), and he was Uncas's dad. Their method of finding their way through the most intricate forest, even after dark, was legendary. Moreover, not many years ago a redskin from Springs, Steve Talkhouse, was offered a lift by a white man in his motor car and told him:

'No thanks, I'm in a hurry.' By which he meant that, following the tracks through woods and fields which only an Indian would know of, he was sure to reach his destination ahead of the motorist.

No Red Indian dish has survived in the local cuisine. Just as well, considering that the redskins, from a culinary viewpoint, are undoubtedly the world's least well-endowed people. One local dish, however, is curious, to say the least: graveyard stew, which is normally fed to those who are seriously ill. It is a broth of bread and milk, simple and quick to make: toast a slice of good bread, butter it, put it into a soup bowl, add salt and pepper and pour on to it a cup of piping hot, but not scalding, milk. An excellent broth for anyone in good health; for a sick person who is up in local traditions, a make-or-break experience.

A group of Shinnecock Indians had been following my words in silence up to this point. But now one of them, the old chief Splendid Canoe, broke in: 'It's not true that nothing survives of our cooking. Succotash is an Indian dish.'

Indeed, he was not wrong: Succotash is an Indian dish made from sweetcorn and lima beans cooked together, nowadays reduced to being a side dish, and often upgraded by substituting buttered and sliced French beans for lima beans.

'Squaw disk is an Indian dish,' said the next one. (This is egg, bacon and the usual sweetcorn.)

'You're right,' I said. 'But it's no great shakes.'

Splendid Canoe coughed and solemnly got to his feet. 'God has given them enough,' he observed, 'but they want the lot. Such are the palefaces.'

This said (quoting from *The Last of the Mohicans*, as also are the words that follow), with silent, elastic steps he moved off into the forest. 'The rest followed him, one by one, in the order so well known as to deserve the name "Indian file".'

Crow Soup

After supper Kafka would go straight to bed until one o'clock. At one he would get down to his writing; at four or five he would return to bed until such time as he had to get up to go to the office. In a letter to his lady friend Felice dated 14 and 15 January 1913, he described his ideal style of living and working: 'I have often thought that for me the best way to live would be settled in the inner recesses of a vast, closed cellar, with all I needed for writing, plus a lamp. Meals would be brought to me, but the food would always have to be kept at a great distance from where I am, outside the outermost door of the cellar. The movement to go and get my food, in my dressing-gown, walking beneath vaults of the cellar, this would be my only excursion. Then I would return to my table, I should eat slowly, with careful concentration, and get straight back to my writing.'

In his biography of Kafka, Max Brod noted that 'there were certain authors (like Hebbel and Grill-parzer) whom Kafka preferred as diarists rather than for their works: or so it seemed to me'. It does not seem to me irreverent to harbour the same thought about Kafka: I mean that his diaries (and letters) are the best of his work.

He was a vegetarian and took little interest in food. He notes, in his diaries, a dinner on New Year's Eve, modest but with its touch of refinement, 'with salsify and spinach, accompanied by a quarter of sherry'; a supper 'with strawberries'; another, in Berlin, with 'rice à la Trautmannsdorf [a dessert nowadays called Rice à l'Impératrice] and a peach'. From Milan he recollects an apple tart eaten 'in the Cortile dei Mercanti', and the beer, which 'smells like beer, tastes like wine'.

However he did perhaps make an understandable exception for soup. 'You say that with the same sort of distaste as if you'd found a hair in your soup,' says a character in one of his stories. And in another story we read: 'He smiles at me as if I were bringing him perhaps the richest of rich soups.'[1]

The surname Kafka, as Max Brod also observes, is of Czech origin and, in its correct transcription as 'Kavka', literally means a crow. Were it not so unattractive a bird, I should say it was a reminder of Kafka's scowling face. 'The flesh of this bird', wrote a nineteenth-century naturalist, 'is repulsive, but it does provide an excellent and very healthy soup.'

[1] 'Unhappiness' and 'A Country Doctor', *Stories* by Franz Kafka, trans. J. A. Underwood.

Cooked Ham with Pineapple

From 1938 . . .

Crushed in the small crowd of customers in the delicatessen, I stood in a brown study, like a horse, awaiting my turn.

From 1938 I was remembering . . . in particular the cooked ham in Trieste. Nowadays nobody knows what cooked ham is, what it can be. In those days you found it everywhere, on the bone, with its pink side of succulent fat which kept the lean side juicy and so tender. But in Trieste it was something else again; Vienna and Prague were two steps off, they had been but one step away. The result was well in evidence in the windows of the delicatessen; it steamed on the counter in the cook shops . . . You have it cut in slices three or four millimetres thick and you throw it good and hot on the slab, and you place beside them a few slices of pineapple, one for each slice of ham. Pork meat, as the Chinese well know, goes well with sweet things. The pineapple takes on the flavour and brown colour of burnt sugar. A novel, exotic flavour which comes from remote Hawaii via Virginia, mother of presidents and all kinds of ham . . .

'A hundred grams of the cooked,' said the customer in front of me. He had a feverish look, his hands trembled as he fingered his jacket.

The shopkeeper, however, was smiling. As usual. He took from a marble slab a squared block of pieces of meat pressed together, of a violent, optimistic rose colour, and prodded it affectionately.

'All lean,' he said as he placed it on the meat slicer.

From the other waiting customers, compacted like the ham in the little shop, there arose a murmur of approval.

The slices, dry as sheets of plastic, piled up on the weighing scales. The shopkeeper laid them down carefully, with the same fingers which, a moment before, had counted out the change on a 10,000-lira note. Ham and microbes.

'One hundred grams exactly,' he concluded, adding a microbe to make up the weight, then wiping his fingers on his publicity apron.

He made up an elegant parcel, and tied it with a ribbon, using a knife to curl up the ends.

The customer slipped his quaking right hand inside his jacket.

But instead of his wallet, what he pulled out was a pistol, and before anyone could stop him he shot the shopkeeper and his wife, who was standing next to him behind the counter.

'This way you will learn', shouted the murderer (for the two poor souls who'd had their brains shot out it was, alas, too late to learn), 'not to accept from your suppliers these blocks of plastic in place of cooked ham, or serve this same plastic to your customers. And I shall kill any customer who accepts plastic in place of cooked ham!'

'You, mate,' he continued, ever more excited, turning the barrel of the still-smoking pistol towards me, 'what is it you wanted to buy?'

'Salted anchovies,' I found myself saying.

'Not cooked ham?'

'Absolutely not. I see that you are a champion of good cooked ham so allow me to give you a piece of advice. Go to Trieste. That's the one place where you have a good chance of still finding authentic cooked ham. Don't wait till tomorrow, go today.'

'OK, mate,' he said, thrusting the pistol back into his inside coat pocket. 'How do I get to the station?'

Several clients vied with each other to direct him to the metro station at the end of the street.

I could tell from the way he spoke and acted that he was a phoney, not only undeserving of authentic cooked ham, about which he had, in fact, made some entirely correct observations, but even of a simple tin of Spam. It was all put on.

In fact, the moment he was out of the shop, the man with the brains blown out and his wife got back on their feet behind the counter, as though nothing untoward had occurred.

'Who's next?'

Sandwich

A notable improvement in the culinary standards of American restaurants is the meritorious achievement (the one and only) of the Mafia gangsters, folk who have always set great store by their food – in fact, a good number of them have been killed off while at table. Joe Cipolla (prophetic name),[1] who came to America from Sicily in 1903 and was chef to three generations of Mafia bosses, dons, big shots, panjandrums, top bananas, grease balls and men of honour, has assembled in his small tome, *The Mafia Cookbook*, the best in his repertoire, from Chicken Valachi to Shot-gun Pigeons, to Capon Al Capone . . .

On the other hand, the habit of the quick bite at midday has given birth to all manner of sandwiches: some of them colossal, many-layered, not easy to handle without practice. 'Americans', says Chandler, 'will eat anything if it is toasted and held together with a couple of toothpicks and has lettuce sticking out of the sides, preferably a little wilted.' Such a sandwich, according to Chandler,

[1] Cipolla means onion. [Translator]

is 'as full of rich flavour as a piece torn off an old shirt'.[2] But there are some excellent ones as well. Among the best are the BLT (the initials for bacon, lettuce and tomato). Between two slices of toast, crisp lettuce leaves, tomato slices and pickled gherkins, a touch of mayonnaise and two or three rashers of fried bacon, crisp as the lettuce. Flying off to distant Paris in *The Spirit of St Louis* on 20 May 1927, Lindbergh who, in order to save fuel, kept the aircraft so low that he felt the ocean spray on his face, had as his only companion a pack of sandwiches.

I think that this word may be included among foreign words in common use, like film and bar, which evade the rules of declension in Italian. Thus I shall write two sandwich and not two sandwiches. But above all, not two sandwicks, as one reads in the agreeable volume by Olindo Guerrini from which we have already quoted, or sandwichs, as we read in Artusi. In those days everybody studied French, while English was still an adventure.

---

[2] Raymond Chandler, *The Long Goodbye*. Raymond Chandler (whose era is characterised by two objects now extinct: the hat and the spittoon) is well known for his analogies. I note one here that relates to eating, one of the very few because Philip Marlowe, a great drinker and smoker, paid scant attention to what he ate: 'He looked at me without haste, without interest, as though he were looking at a left-over hunk of boiled meat' (*The Big Sleep*).

Buttered Salsify

When the beans are excellent, the butter absolutely fresh, and the pepper is ground directly on to the plate, a helping of string beans with butter and pepper is undoubtedly one of the best starters. Those grown around Naples are (still?) the best in the world: slender as vermicelli, flavoursome, tender, and of course without a trace of string. Alas, the moment you get away from Naples you're bound to run into stringy string beans. This world is full of mysteries. Here is one of them: why do nurserymen continue to plant beans with strings in them? Stringless beans of top quality do exist and yet, when the season comes round, *thousands of nurserymen sow stringy beans*.

It's a mystery that may be explained through inertia: once there have been stringy beans in that patch (for centuries), the grower continues to harvest its seed from one year to the next, and the possibility of making a change never crosses his mind. Only now and then does someone come along and say: 'What if I tried to buy seed from some of the stringless sort?' If he has it in him to pass from thought to action, the following spring he picks stringless beans and the sorry spell that weighed on the bean plot is lifted. But these must be extremely rare cases, otherwise over all the centuries since mankind has been eating runner beans, the strings would have disappeared a good while back.

Poor-quality greens and poor-quality fruit are not only difficult to replace but in fact have a tendency to spread like weeds and take over the patches of their betters. Tasteless 'vanilla' oranges have mounted a first attack on classic oranges, an attack that has, thank goodness, failed. But then those uncouth 'blood' oranges have achieved success and spread far and wide; in them the flavour of the original has quite been lost. Somebody might argue that there's no accounting for tastes. I shall agree with that person, just as I should if a necrophiliac (who lusts after corpses) quoted the same saying at me. In oranges one notices another prevailing tendency of fruit-growers: that of arriving at an ever-larger product, regardless of the fact that as a rule it is the smaller fruit that is the better. Salsify, which the Anglo-Saxons call an oyster plant, is a vanishing species. Those delicious Regina Claudia plums (after turning seventy, d'Annunzio called *Susina Claudia* – the Claudia plum – the last of his lovers) are disappearing from the markets, to be replaced by plums that taste of nothing, or taste sour.

This loss of sensitivity is now widespread. Those who turn up the volume of their radios and television sets full blast and take their portable radios on to the beach, and only eat the most widely advertised processed cheeses, use vanilla essence instead of vanilla sticks, throw their cigarette stubs on to the tracks on the metro, haven't learnt about queuing, dedicate their latest novel 'To my wife, who lovingly typed out the manuscript', blush if their grandpa ties his napkin round his neck, have insisted that prison screws, street sweepers, firemen, the blind and the deaf be called security agents, highway cleansing officers or, worse, ecological officers, anti-incendiary specialists, the visually- and otically-challenged, call an earthquake a seismic occurrence, greet their office colleagues with 'Have a nice day', these are also the ones who on the office outing to Lake Como gather in a close-knit group round an untuned guitar, probably below decks, and make the round trip between Como and Bellagio without so much as a glance at the water, the shore, the villas, the mountains, the sky. In the evening, on leaving the station, they buy a kilo of sour plums and that's the end of the trip.

These are the same people who think that roast-chestnut sellers, hot-dog pedlars and market stalls are unsightly, while in fact they turn any anonymous site in the city into an attractive, human, therapeutic place for the usual neuroses. You stallholders (male and female), you landlords of old *osterie* that have not been 'done up' with bowling alleys, you carpenters' shops, you knife-grinders, umbrella sellers, chair caners, water-melon sellers, purveyors of chestnut-cake, lupins, cooked pears, you who still live down by the railings, stuck between the privy and the trash cans, or out in Grottsville, should be entitled to the gratitude of your fellow-citizens. Instead of which some pillar of the community has even observed: 'If the Town Hall listened to me, we'd ban roast chestnuts.'

Unfortunately it is the wrong-headed who inherit the earth. Lacking the energy of Ralph Nader,[1] all we can do is drink ourselves into oblivion.

To drink, yes, but in moderation. W. C. Fields (William Claude Dukenfield), a fantastic juggler, and later an American screen comic (he made his debut escaping from home and doing his juggling act aged eleven), drank too much. He ended up an alcoholic. Shortly before he died, on Christmas Day 1946, he said: 'I've drunk so copiously to the health of others that finally I've lost my own.'

Salsify is usually cooked in butter. The roots are scraped clean, leaving the first three or four

[1] Ralph Nader is the creator (from nothing) in the United States of a very active and worthwhile organisation that conducts research and mounts appeals against violations of the public interest by whomsoever. His family was Arab, immigrants from the Lebanon (his father owned a modest restaurant and possibly regaled his customers with delicious frogs in coriander, the Beirut speciality), and he is a product of the particular air which (even now, fortunately) is breathed in that great country.

centimetres of leaf. You cut them into approximately eight-centimetre chunks and immerse them in water to which you have added lemon or vinegar to prevent them from going black; then you toss them into boiling water (to which you've added a level spoonful of flour and two of vinegar for each litre of water, and salt as required), cover and set them to simmer until they are tender (to test, squeeze between two fingers). Then you drain them and sauté them in butter, seasoning them with salt and black pepper to taste. Truly salsify is the oyster among vegetables and, like all oysters, it demands champagne as an accompaniment.

Savoury delicacies like the oyster plant cooked in butter need to be eaten in ideal conditions. The room must be south-facing, get plenty of sun, and be well lit after dark, avoiding neon lighting at all costs as this gives the food a macabre hue, and avoiding darkness too, as this diminishes the sense of taste and smell. Candle light will do if this improves the situation. The floor must give warmth, that is, it must be wooden (a marble floor in a dining room or restaurant is a serious mistake). The table should be large (even if we are on our own), covered with the most pristine of tablecloths. Upholstered chairs should have upholstered arm-rests to rest one's arms every now and then, as they are kept very busy during the meal. There should be no more than five at the table, otherwise the group tends to split up like an amoeba into two sub-groups conversing independently of each other and making for mutual disturbance. Scents should be reduced to a minimum, lest they blend unsatisfactorily with the aroma of the food.

As to the number of the diners, I find confirmation in Archestratus, a strange Sicilian poet and gourmet who lived three centuries before Christ. As often happens to worthy souls, he was unjustly mocked by his contemporaries who nicknamed him the Glutton, the Ape of Sardanapalus, the Nifty Kitchen Hand, the Top Scullion, the Hesiod of the Plate-lickers, the Theognis of the Greedy. So we are told by Domenico Scinà in the foreword to the Italian translation of what survives of Archestratus's *Gastronomia*. Here are the lines regarding the number of diners: 'Of delicious meats let but one table / Accommodate everybody; but three or four / Or not more than five should be the number of the company: / Because were they more, it would be a meal / For predators, for mercenary troops.'

Lastly, a spotless napkin. Time was when napkins were set out on the plates, folded in various fantastical ways, in the shape of animals, a head-dress, a ship or whatever; at the end of the meal they were refolded, this time as a letter is folded and slipped into a personal envelope made of cloth, embroidered by one's aunt. (Trattorias, *pensions* and hostels would provide paper envelopes, with an advertisement for some make of mineral water, and a blank rectangle in which the customer would write his name, surname, degrees and all the letters after his name.) Otherwise the napkins were rolled up and stuck in a nickel-plated brass ring, or, for the rich, one of silver gilt, engraved with their initials. Which is a reminder that in an age even more remote the rich would use porcelain chamber pots, exquisitely decorated, which certain persons of questionable taste will use nowadays for a salad bowl. The Sun King probably kept in his commode a precious potty in chased gold. But, as they say in Rome, a piss-pot is always a piss-pot. And dirty napkins are something to be put into the wash rather than into an envelope or a ring. If napkins cannot be changed with every meal, far better to place a box of paper napkins on the table.

Borage Fritters

Pontormo has left a short diary in which practically all he notes down relates to what he's painting and what he's eating.

Saturday night had supper with Piero, fish from the Arno, ricotta, eggs and artichokes.

Thursday night lettuce salad and caviar and an egg.

Saturday went to the inn: salad and fish eggs and goat's cheese and I felt well. [Fish eggs is an omelette which, when folded over on itself, acquires the shape of a fish. The term is still used today in Sicily.]

Wednesday I dined off 14 *once* of bread, pork chine, an endive salad and goat's cheese and dried figs.

These are simple dishes from traditional working-class cuisine, so different from the highly complicated menus which have come down to us from Renaissance times: endless courses overladen with spices, sugar, cinnamon, etc.

Thursday I dined off 15 *once* of bread.
Friday 14 *once* of bread.
Saturday I did not dine.

Sometimes Pontormo would dine off nothing but bread (but of good quality); sometimes he skipped a meal. Or ate by himself.

Sunday and Monday I cooked myself a piece of veal bought for me by Ba[stiano] and I stayed here at home for two days drawing and those three nights I dined on my own.

He was orphaned young and was made a ward of court. 'A morose and solitary young man', as Vasari[1] describes him, saying that 'the room in which he slept and occasionally worked was reached by a wooden ladder, and once he had entered, he would haul it up with a pulley, so that nobody could come up to visit him without his knowledge and consent'.

On the table in the *Supper at Emmaus*, in the Uffizi, two tempting filled rolls are to be seen, marvellously depicted. Had Pontormo been born later, every menu in his diary might have been a most beautiful still life.

That evening I dined off the remains of a stew and pork chine left over from Thursday, cooked borage, 9 *once* of rosemary bread.

[1] Giorgio Vasari, 'Life of Iacopo da Puntormo, Florentine Painter', in *Lives of the Artists*.

Borage features more than once in Pontormo's menus: cooked (in not much water), in a salad – there is even a salad made from borage flowers which are quite beautiful, pink and blue on the same plant. The leaves are hairy and add flavour to a salad. Borage is little used nowadays, except in Liguria where borage fritters are on sale in Genoa from the fried-food stalls on the harbour front, and in the oriental market.

From an old, anonymously written cookbook, *L'arte della cucina, manuale completo per i cuochi e le famiglie*, I transcribe the recipe for the almost forgotten borage fritter:

'Prepare a fairly thick batter with two handfuls of flour, a half glass of white wine, a spoonful of oil and a pinch of salt, beating these ingredients thoroughly. Take some borage leaves, wash them in fresh water, let them drain, chop them up and add them to the above-mentioned batter; then mix this up some more and throw the mixture a spoonful at a time into a pan with sizzling oil, thus making the fritters, which are to be served sprinkled with sugar.

'Instead of chopping the borage, it may be cooked whole-leaf, after dipping the leaves in the batter.'

Tiella

I stopped in Lecce a few years ago and got out of the taxi in Piazza Mazzini, a vast, dreary rectangle smothered in new buildings that were much too tall. In the middle of the piazza a great 'monumental' fountain was under construction, even if nobody was then at work on it, a hideous thing in Carrara marble. Design and supervision: local council engineers' department.

I stopped a passer-by and asked him what did he think the fountain was costing.

He didn't know. I later discovered it was going to cost a bomb.

I also asked the passer-by, who was eyeing me suspiciously, how come, in his view, the fountain was being constructed out of Carrara marble, which was expensive and totally out of character with a city built like this one with the most beautiful local stone (the old quarter at least).

He didn't know.

Then I asked him to direct me to a trattoria where I would get a decent meal.

I saw a complete change come over him: the nightmare was over with all those questions about the fountain and he started beaming. Faced with normal questions, he reverted to being a normal citizen; he became positively civil and hospitable.

'Go to Mamma Roma's in Viale Otranto; that's the place for a good meal, mark my words.'

And in fact at Mamma Roma's, after a few spoonfuls of artichoke soup I had quite forgotten about Piazza Mazzini and its ghastly fountain. Lecce had turned once again into the wonderful old Hispanic city, with its kitchen gardens in red soil and their tiny leaves of phosphorescent green, the Galatina endive, the marzipan sweets turned out by cloistered nuns, the old pâtisseries in which the customer, confronted with the choice between an almond milk and an iced coffee, is in a complete dilemma thanks to the absolute ecstasy of both these drinks. The iced coffee is a boiling hot espresso on the rocks, that is, poured into a glass containing ice cubes and sugar: it freezes while preserving the flavour of the piping-hot coffee.

The artichoke soup is simplicity itself; a trainee chef could start here in the assurance of success.

Allow one artichoke per person and cut each into eight pieces once the outer leaves have been removed. Toss the chokes into boiling water, allowing one bowlful per person. Add salt and when, after some fifteen minutes, the artichokes are cooked, pour the soup into the bowls and add a little olive oil and black pepper to taste.

There is another soup from the Puglie which is also excellent – pasta and potato.

Enough for five. In 100 ml olive oil fry a finely chopped onion and a clove of garlic; add 600 g diced potato and steep them without letting them fry; add a glass of white wine and finish off with flavourings: parsley and a little celery, both chopped, oregano, marjoram, rosemary, a bay leaf and nutmeg.

Go very easy on the nutmeg, that is a general rule: a pinch is too much – no more than a touch, a smidgen, a tad, a whisper. The French say *un soupçon*, a suspicion: in a word, you must suspect that it is present, but not be sure.

Cover the potatoes and simmer them slowly, adding stock. When they are almost done add the pasta (225 g short macaroni-type pasta) already parboiled and drained. Take the soup off the boil – it should not reduce too much.

(Fellini has had the bright idea of altering the flavour of a soup with a certain finesse – not every soup, of course: add a spoonful of whisky. Try it in a thick vegetable soup. When the irretrievable passage of time has turned even his films into comics, Fellini will still be remembered, and maybe obtain blessings, for this simple but positive contribution to the art of eating well.)

I have been back to Lecce but I have not been to see whether the fountain was finished. Trattoria Roma is still there but Mamma Roma, now widowed, has retired. Her immediate successors did not, it seems, come up to scratch. Some months ago the place was taken over by Cosimo (Cosimino) Malerba, who brought along with him the chef he had when he was still running the hotel restaurant . . . I mention this all too frequent alternation of highs and lows in order to stress what little store is often to be set by restaurant guides. Those who blindly follow the guide still patronise the hotel, expecting to find the good cooking of Cosimino who is now here instead.

If it is a spring lunchtime order the *tiella*, a shallow oven dish stuffed with potatoes, toma-toes, onion, garlic, artichokes, courgettes, all chopped, and mussels in their brine, a little rice, salt, pepper, oil, and as much water as it takes to prevent the oil sizzling and to cook the rice and vegetables. *Tiella* is baked in the oven, which provides heat below and above – the top layer of potatoes has to roast.

'When I started I was cooking for six covers, now I'm doing fifty,' says Cosimino with justi-fiable pride. The place has remained unpreten-tious, but the tablecloths are clean, like the chef's outfit.

A customer seated before a plate of pasta and beans asks for cheese.

'As a rule, cheese is not put on pasta and beans,' says Cosimino politely.

'Well, I', says the customer, 'put cheese even in my coffee.'

'As you wish . . .'

Good cooking and courtesy, even towards those who wish to sprinkle their pasta and beans with cheese: success ought to be assured. Even though nowadays success is more easily assured with a ghastly *mise-en-scène* of garish colours, blinding lights, mock-rustic chairs, hideous pictures on the walls and lousy cooking.

Spezzatino alla zurighese with rösti

'What', asked the teacher, interrupting his passage between the desks, 'is wrong with the standard Italian *spezzatino* or stew?' He gave a slight backward tilt to the snowy-white chef's hat which was the symbol of his office and, to obtain his pupils' attention, tapped twice on a desk with the wooden spoon he was holding. Not that there was any need: they were all hanging on his words.

'The tomato, that's what's wrong. The time has come to say quite frankly that meat and tomato do not form an ideal combination. There is something facile, overweight, common in this conjunction. As a result, I should treat Bolognese sauce with a measure of reserve. (Not to mention that dish from Piacenza, *pìcula ad caval*, which lies halfway between a meat sauce and a stew, but let's skip the details.)

'Let us now turn to the two best-known tomato-free *spezzatini*: French *blanquette de veau* and the Zürich version, *Geschnitzeltes Zürcherart*. Leaving aside the former, to which we shall return in due course, let us consider the latter.'

He went to the blackboard and wrote:

Veal (rump): 700 g, thinly sliced
One onion
Lard: 40 g
Flour: about 10 g
White wine: 100 ml
Stock: 100 ml
Cream: 4–6 spoonfuls
Cognac: a small glassful

At the bottom he added, in Spanish as usual: '*Sal y pimienta al gusto* [salt and pepper to taste]'. This was one of his foibles. He wiped his hands on the duster, grasped the spoon again, and resumed his saunter amid the desks.

'Cut up the slices of veal into pieces of approximately three by two centimetres. Sauté the onion in the lard. Turn up the flame a little and toss the meat into the frying pan, turning it constantly with the wooden spoon until it has browned. Note well: the wooden spoon is the cook's Number One Utensil ... Take the pan off the heat, on with the cognac now. Set it alight, that is, quickly tip the pan so as to bring the liquid to the edge, heating the edge on the flame. Then sprinkle on the flour and add the wine and stock. Simmer for a further two minutes, season and pour in the cream, giving a final stir.'

He returned to his desk and asked the class: 'Now, *Geschnitzeltes Zürcherart* – what is it served with?'

'With *rösti*,' chorused the students.

'What kind of *rösti*?'

The students looked at each other doubtfully.

'With *rösti* from the Canton of Aargau or from the Canton of Basel? From the Canton of Bern or the Canton of Glarus or the Canton of Zürich?'

Clearly the teacher went to the heart of every problem. *Rösti* are made with boiled potatoes allowed to cool, then peeled and grated with a special very coarse grater. They are fried in a frying pan, in the form of an omelette. Cook on a low heat in a lidded pan, frequently shaking the pan to prevent the potatoes from catching. After fifteen minutes the 'omelette' is flipped over and the other side cooked for the same length of time. They are fried in butter with small pieces of bacon (Aargau), in butter with finely chopped onions which have first been sautéed (Basel), in butter and lard (Bern), and in butter with Schabzieger cheese, a cheese with herbs – we might make do with Gorgonzola – in the Canton of Glarus. The Zürich *rösti* are like the Basel ones except that the potatoes are raw when grated.

'Any *rösti* will do,' said the teacher, 'but as the *spezzatino* is from Zürich, I should go for Zürich *rösti*. The wooden spoon . . .'

He was interrupted by the bell. End of class. The students went out into the corridor and a suspicion of sulphur hung about the classroom.

Many years ago, strolling past the Excelsior, on Venice's Lido, around lunchtime, I came upon a mouth-watering smell emerging from the kitchens, along with a weird singsong in the bowels of the hotel. Behind the thick grating of a window on a level with the pavement could be glimpsed, way below, a scene from hell: red-hot kitchen ranges, glowing coals, griddles, ovens, flames, steam, smoke; and here and there the chefs and their assistants were going back and forth, dressed in nothing but a woollen blanket wound twice round their middles, flushed from the heat of the fires, armed with huge forks like devils. What the singsong was about were the orders which arrived all distorted, through a speaking-tube, from the floor above where the clients ate their meals in peace, little realising they were sitting atop an inferno. Cooks, according to Joyce, are spawn of the devil: 'God made food, the devil made cooks.'[1]

Joyce pops up unexpectedly from behind a bush if anyone goes in search of him in the Friedhof Fluntern, the splendid Zürich cemetery. He is seated on a chair of bronze, with a bronze stick, a bronze shin sportively resting on a bronze thigh. His spectacles have no lenses, and the only thing missing is a bottle of his favourite Fendant de Sion at the foot of the chair, within easy reach. This is a wine, Saul Steinberg tells us, which can be drunk even without food: a wine to chat by.

I have long been in two minds as to whether it was right to publish the recipe for *pìcula ad caval*, a

[1] James Joyce, *Ulysses*, 1922.

mysterious and most beautiful name for anyone who is not from Piacenza, but which may now lose some of its magic. And I am bound to warn people of delicate sensibilities not to read the recipe that follows.

Take onion, carrot, celery, a little garlic and parsley, chop them up finely and sauté this flavoursome mixture in butter. Throw on to this a kilo of minced horsemeat and fry it for about ten minutes. Add chopped tomatoes and a bay leaf, stir well and lastly, after seasoning with salt and pepper q.s. (*quantum sufficit*), pour over the lot a half litre of red wine, cover the *pìcula ad caval*, now shorn of its mystery, and leave to simmer slowly. A distant, almost imperceptible whinny will warn the person who is familiar with horses that the dish is now cooked. (It is eaten with polenta.)

Carasau Bread

Although bakeries seem to be making a come-back, bread is everywhere on the way out, and the Italian expression 'good, like bread' is beginning to lose its meaning. Before long we Italians shall be saying, as the English do, 'Good as gold'. Only a few years ago in Paris you would eat a delicious baguette, and it was always fresh in the restaurants, even in the evening.

Today there are very few bakers in Paris who make bread the way they used to, and the Parisians, who have mounted protests for so many other things, do not protest over the poor-quality bread, nor do they organise an immense sit-in on Place de la Concorde in order to force the government . . .

Dreams. Third-rate bread will win the battle over first-rate bread. Only private citizens will be able to recapture the taste of bread as it was once upon a time, kneading the right flour with the right yeast in accordance with the rules nowadays flouted by the commercial bakeries, and baking the rolls (or the various flat-breads or pizzas) in a little wood-burning oven that will be built in their country villas (not a huge outlay). It could become fashionable, after the success of open-air barbecues, and we shall revert to seeing in cookbooks the recipes for the 200 different kinds of bread – from the huge honey-coloured loaves from Matera to the thin leaves of Sardinian *carasau* bread – recorded *viva voce* by a new generation of master-bakers.

For a start I question one at the door of his little shop.

'Tell me, sir, do you have an official qualification as a baker? Did you learn the craft in a school or have you picked it up working with a master of the trade, just as once upon a time the greatest painters, sculptors and architects did?'

'I learned from my father. Nowadays, in town, you need a diploma.'

'Don't people complain that bread is no longer what it used to be?'

'No, just so long as the bread is white.'

'Why is natural yeast no longer used, as this makes for better-quality bread?'

'Because natural yeast makes for more work: the kneading process has to be repeated several times. Therefore we use what is known as beer-yeast.'

'Did you know that the ancient Egyptians used their feet to knead the dough?'

'. . . ?'

'Grapes, too, used to be trodden down to make wine. Our ancestors used their feet more than we do. As, by the bye, monkeys still do.'

'. . . ?'

'Is a wood-burning oven better than those run on electricity or oil?'

'Of course. The embers give the bread its own special smell and taste.'

'Is it true, as some bakers have told me, that wood-burning ovens are banned for reasons of hygiene?'

The master-baker goes and takes his licence off the wall: he shows it to me – it is in good order and permits the use of a wood-burning oven.

'No, what's spelling the end of wood-burning ovens is the difficulty in obtaining faggots. Nobody goes into the woods any more to cut them, and even if they did, they'd be too expensive.'

An elderly man, a fat man whose obesity did not suggest well-being and joviality, had stopped close by and seemed to be following our conversation attentively.

'You see,' I said to the master-baker, 'bread is a topic of universal interest. This gentleman represents the man in the street,' and in fact he was carrying a haversack over his shoulder. 'If the question of bread interests him, that can only mean that it is a matter of some importance, isn't it?' said I, turning to the man with the haversack.

The man seemed to come to life; he drew from his pocket (a somewhat bedraggled one) a pink printed note and politely handed it to me.

'Dear Sir, Madam. Nature created me DEAF AND DUMB and my only means of existence is my neighbour's generosity. So I appeal to your good nature. Thank you kindly.'

To bring us luck, let us conclude with the recipe for *carasau* bread, that is, a dry, biscuit-type of bread that is baked twice over (*pistoccu*); it is also known as *pane de domo* (household bread), *pane tostu* (toasted), *pane de vresa* (that is, cut in two, inasmuch as a *vresa* means a half loaf), as it is made around Nuoro in Sardinia – even though we know perfectly well that to make *carasau* bread the recipe by itself is not enough. Never mind . . .

The flour, of the hard-grain variety (such as is used for pasta), is kneaded and mixed with a little bran, using warm water, salt and natural yeast. Once you have a dough similar to bread dough, you make a cylindrical shape that is then cut into slices of identical size, sufficient for each one to be rolled out into a disc of about forty centimetres in diameter, and some two to three millimetres thick. Using a good length of cloth, folded over each disc concertina-style, the discs are laid one on top of the other and left to rest for half an hour.

The discs are put one at a time into the wood-burning oven, heated to 250° C, for a mere twenty seconds (in order to dry them) and are then stacked again, each one separated, as before, by the cloth.

Once again the discs are put into the oven, until they swell up like balloons. Now they are removed and a different hand (as a rule it takes three women to make *carasau* bread) runs a knife through the side of the balloon, presses on it to deflate it and slices it all the way round to produce a pair of discs which are stacked (with those that follow) one on top of the other, the inner sides uppermost. On the topmost disc a cloth is laid along with a flat chunk of heavy timber to keep the discs flattened out.

Lastly, the discs are put back into the oven with a metal shovel (formerly the traditional wooden shovel was used), one at a time, inner side facing up, and are jiggled about in front of the fire at the back of the oven, so as to brown them and make them crisp without singeing them. A stack is made with the finished discs, this time without any cloth or weight.

Quite an operation, as you see. In the days when each family baked its own bread at home, the expression 'time is money' had not yet spread, like a dark cloud, above the horizon. Now that at Bergamo they have invented a machine for making polenta, they will have found some way of making a machine that turns out *carasau* bread, which will of course look like *carasau* bread, but will not taste like it. Luckily on the island there survive teams of little old women – God bless 'em! – able to offer (but only for a little longer, as nobody will take their place) this marvellous spectacle of craftsmanly know-how which, out of flour, water, salt and fire, brings forth the magical sunshine of *carasau* bread.

Carasau bread will keep a long time if stored in a dry place. It is eaten as bread and is excellent with milk. Used as *lasagna* (dipped for a few seconds in boiling water and placed in layers in a pan with grated *pecorino* cheese, tomato sauce, and a poached egg for a crown), it makes a typical dish from Nuoro: *pane frattau*.

> *Beatus ille homo*
> *Qui sedet in sua domo*
> *Et sedet post fornacem*
> *Et habet bonam pacem!*[1]

[1] Lines written by Joseph von Eichendorff: 'Happy the man / Who sits at home, / Ensconced by the stove, / And enjoying goodly peace.'

Boarding-house pastina in brodo

'What did you have for lunch?'

'*Pastina in brodo* . . . small butterfly shapes. And cheese.'

'And this evening?'

'This evening marrow-bone with frozen peas.'

'Any fruit?'

'I don't know . . . Perhaps an apple.'

'What kind of apple?'

'Golden Delicious. And a glass or two of wine.'

'Any dessert?'

'No. That's enough as it is. On Sunday: profiteroles.'

'Anything instead of *pastina in brodo*?'

'Sometimes tagliatelle: plain with butter, or maybe in a tomato sauce. Never a Bolognese.'

'Why not?'

'I don't care for it, neither does my fellow-lodger.'

'What does your fellow-lodger do?'

'Chauffeur . . . for a company director.'

'Do the hours work out?'

'Yes, more or less.'

'What time do you have supper?'

'Seven-thirty.'

'Any liqueur to finish?'

'No . . . almost never.'

'Is the pepper in a grinder or ready-ground?'

'Ready-ground.'

'The napkin: is it kept in a pouch or in a ring?'

'A ring.'

'Do you remember a special meal, something out of the ordinary?'

'No.'

'Truffles?'

'It's a while since I last ate them: something like . . . twenty years.'

'Where did you last eat them?'

'In a trattoria off Corso Buenos Aires. On a Milanese veal cutlet.'

'After your meal, a wee nap?'

'I haven't time.'

'Does your landlady eat with the two of you?'

'Yes. She brings in a tray and serves up. If anything's left over, it's eaten the following day: fried rice, meatballs . . .'

'Fish?'

'Very seldom. Once she made a mixed fry-up with scampi and baby squid.'

'When was that?'

'Can't remember.'

'Coffee?'

'Not always. When it's wanted.'

'Toothpicks?'

'Don't use them.'

'Are the chairs upholstered?'

'Yes.'

'Comfortable?'

'Fairly.'

'What's the upholstery like?'

'Flower-patterned; dull colours.'

'The light?'

'A chandelier with several bulbs, and crystal droplets.'

'Pictures on the walls?'

'Yes, a view of Milan: Vicolo dei Lavandai, at Porta Ticinese. Also a couple of flower paintings.'

'Oils?'

'Yes. At least . . .'

'The *pastina in brodo* – always those butterfly shapes?'

'Butterflies . . . Yes . . . Come to think of it, balls too . . . and stars . . .'

A nightmare. I sit down at a table in the trattoria, covered with a tablecloth sullied with wine of unidentified denomination, tomato sauce, Bolognese ditto, olive oil by no means extra-virgin, and vinegar (not wine vinegar). A sweaty waiter in a soiled jacket mops his brow with a dirty napkin normally clutched under his armpit, brushes off the larger crumbs from the soiled tablecloth, with the same cloth makes a pretence of wiping off the lipstick from the chipped rim of the purple tumblers. In the glass containers the 'pepper' is antique dust, the salt, being damp, is cemented into blocks. In the plastic basket the bread is not fresh; it has already witnessed a number of meals without taking any part: it will end up on some Milanese cutlet (of elderly beef). The table rocks. The shouts of the customers and the racket of the cutlery on the plates make it necessary for everyone to speak at the top of their voices if they are to be heard. From the door to the toilet, which is in full view, there comes the noise of the flush . . .

As a rule the degradation is unremitting. It even affects the inn sign: the owner rubs out Osteria, or Trattoria, or Wine and Cooked Food, and puts instead Hostaria.

A totally unpredictable sign, which shows how far certain 'fantasies' can stretch, features in the following stanzas from Baudelaire's 'Bouffonneries'.

Un cabaret folâtre
sur la route de Bruxelles à Uccle

Vous qui raffolez des squelettes
Et des emblèmes détestés,
Pour épicer les voluptés,
(Fût-ce de simples omelettes!)

Vieux Pharaon, ô Monselet!
Devant cette enseigne imprévue,
J'ai rêvé de vous: À la vue
Du Cimetière, Estaminet![1]

[1] Charles Baudelaire, *Œuvres Complètes*. 'A mad cabaret / on the road from Brussels to Uccle': You who can't have enough of skeletons / And loathsome symbols, / To add spice to your lusts, / (Be they for nothing but an omelette!) // You old Pharaoh, Monselet! / Before this unexpected sign, / I thought of you: / Cemetery View, Café!

Even cooking, if it has to be done day in day out, can become a nightmare. Parisians and Romans from Trastevere take their cook-wife and the rest of the family for a meal out more frequently than most. For a change of flavours, too.

Otherwise there is nothing for it but to follow the Veronese painter Fra Girolamo who 'so as not to fret about what he was going to eat every day would cook a great pot of beans on Monday to last him the week'.[2]

Or else like St Nikolaus von Flüe, who lived in a hermitage for nineteen years without ever touching a morsel.

'Impossible,' someone will object.

For these unbelievers here is the recipe for boarding-house *pastina in brodo*.

[2] Giorgio Vasari, *op. cit.*, 'Lives of Fra Jocondo and Liberale and Others from Verona'.

Bring the broth (thin but fatty) to boiling point in a none-too-clean aluminium saucepan. Toss in the *pastina* (star shapes). Get on the phone to a girlfriend and keep chatting for twice the length of time normally needed to cook the *pastina*. Turn off the gas, and when the soup is almost cold bring it to the table and serve it out in stone-cold soup bowls, wishing the company *'Buon appetito'*.

'Thanks. Same to you.'

Nikolaus von Flüe was a venerable Swiss hermit. After abandoning his wife and their ten children, who nevertheless went to attend him on his deathbed, he lived the life of a solitary in the hermitage at Ranft not far from the town of Stans, near the Lake of Lucerne, cradle of the Confederation. He could neither read nor write. In the mornings he prayed, in the afternoons he would visit the local clergymen. He could be seen walking with a rosary in one hand and a stick in the other. He skipped meals. In 1841, when a civil war was about to erupt among the eight cantons that then made up Switzerland, over the admission of two new cantons to the Confederation, Freiburg and Solothurn, the saint managed to avoid the disaster, sending a message of peace to Stans, where the cantonal representatives were assembled (Diet of Stans). The relationship between a faster and a Diet could not but be of the best. In 1947 Nikolaus von Flüe became the saintly protector of Catholic Switzerland.

Diet Cookery, or Cuisine minceur

Paul Bocuse, the best-known of modern French chefs, has said: 'Michel Guérard is the man among us who has the greatest measure of fantasy.' Guérard is the chef who more than any other embodies the new trends in French cuisine, a cuisine which, without turning its back on *haute cuisine*, aims to take account of calorie counts, vitamins, cholesterol, those changes which the rhythm of modern living introduces into human behaviour.

'Barely a quarter of a century ago,' writes Joseph Wechsberg in an exhaustive profile on Guérard,[1] 'Fernand Point defined for me the secret of *haute cuisine* in these words: "Butter, butter, butter, and lashings of time." '

Guérard's *cuisine minceur* is a light cuisine, enjoyable and non-fattening. What Guérard tries to do and succeeds in doing is to translate the recipes of traditional *haute cuisine* into non-fattening versions, eliminating as far as possible butter, cream, egg yolks, etc., a seemingly impossible task but

[1] 'La nature des choses', the *New Yorker*, 28 June 1975.

one which is, at least partially, a success thanks to his flair for innovation.

This is how Guérard describes to Wechsberg an important chapter in this enterprise. 'I wanted to make a *minceur* version of *blanquette de veau*, a delicious traditional French dish, of braised veal bound with a creamy sauce made from meat stock, butter, flour, egg yolks and cream. Delicious but heavy, even if one tries to go easy on the sauce.

'After trimming the fat off the meat, I placed the slices on a colander in the saucepan, on the bottom of which I had put a mixture of vegetables: carrots, watercress, celery from Verona, and button mushrooms, with no liquid added.[2] Once the lid was clamped down on the pan, the meat was cooked in the aromatic steam from the vegetables as the juices from the meat dripped on to them.

'I made the sauce by blending the juices from the cooking with lemon juice and a little of my white cheese, a special sort of cheese that seems to be a cross between Greek feta and cottage cheese. This white cheese is very low in calories and may be whisked up like cream.

'A helping of my *blanquette minceur* contains fewer than two hundred calories, in contrast with the thousand calories in traditional *blanquette*. I served the two versions to a panel of experts. They were all agreed that the *minceur* version had a better, more authentic flavour.'

In his cooking Guérard generally uses little salt and plenty of green peppercorns (fresh, preserved in water). More than an inventor, he regards himself as a regenerator, one who brings back into use things which were widely used once upon a time (the Maya used to cook in steam). He might be set down as a disciple of Archestratus, who could not abide the over-seasoning that his contemporaries went in for. 'Inopportune and excessive / Are, I find, those other preparations / With all that cheese, that oil and fat, / As if

---

[2] I fear that unless liquid (stock) is added the thing will go up in smoke. It's all right as a concept.

preparing a meal for cats.' His recipe for *amia*, a Mediterranean fish of the tuna family, is exemplary: 'Prepare it in fig leaves / With oregano just a little, and no cheese / Indeed no other fat; when you have it thus prepared / Simply, amid those leaves / Wrap it up, and bind it with a reed. / Then place it in the embers, / And be attentive to the time / To ensure it is well baked, and take care / Not to let it burn.'[3]

Le Pot-au-Feu is the name of the first modest restaurant opened by Guérard at the start of his career. Although located at Asnières, a Paris in-

[3] Archestratus, *op. cit.*

dustrial suburb, the place became famous at once. In his bible, *La Grande Cuisine Minceur*, Guérard makes frequent use of the Italian expression *'al dente'*, which may be interpreted as a homage paid by French *nouvelle cuisine* to our own Italian cooking, which for a long time was ill considered precisely because of its simplicity, its artlessness. To Italian cookery 'everyone must of necessity revert sooner or later', says Alberto Savinio in his *Souvenirs*, 'after every dubious, every disastrous incursion whether among the locust-eaters or among those who dine on quintessences.'

An overabundant lady came puffing up to the master chef at Le Pot-au-Feu as he was 'composing' his famous *pot-au-feu*.

'Monsieur Guérard,' she said, 'shall I have to bid a final farewell to those slices of home-baked bread spread with salted butter from Normandy?'

'My dear madam,' replied the master chef, 'I have not to this day succeeded in realising the *minceur* version of a slice of bread and butter; but I've not given up trying.'

Wechsberg, who had just enjoyed an excellent *minceur* dinner, was chuckling with satisfaction.

'When I got up from the table I almost felt as though I had not eaten at all.'

A curious and ingenious method to slim whilst eating one's fill was dreamed up a few years ago by certain American models, who teamed up with a solitary worm. The idea seems beyond criticism, but if the worm diet has not caught on that must mean it had some drawback. Anyway, every rapid-slimming system is harmful and above all ineffective because fat, when it is shed too quickly, is regained just as rapidly. (And far be it for women to model themselves on models. Venus was no beanpole.)

Let us remember, finally, that dieting is not simply a matter of what one eats. As Mességué says: 'A good stew eaten among real friends goes down a lot better than a forlorn diet-leek soup eaten alone in the kitchen.'

High spirits at table are a vital requisite for good digestion. Court jesters sat at the king's table for precisely this purpose. A wise institution. The opposite of our business lunch today, an institution devoid of wisdom, unless we look at our fellow-diners and see clowns.

PART TWO

Home Cooking

A quite distinctive cuisine, not assessable within the normal parameters, which might be defined as the counterpart of canteen cookery, is home cooking: just as Mama (or Auntie) makes it. For the guests this may even mean lousy cooking, but for the household it is something special, which does no harm, which protects, which, in its absence, is recollected with tears in the eye. 'When my mother kept insisting, "Go on, take another dollop of *fettuccine*" (her own *fettuccine*),' observed Ennio Flaiano, 'I would just get irritated. What wouldn't I give now to hear that invitation again and have those *fettuccine* in front of me!'

As I had a German mother who had spent many years in Tuscany, for me domestic cuisine was partly German, partly Tuscan, an agreeable alternation. As Tuscan cookery is all too familiar, what I shall give here are certain dishes from German home cooking, an aid to varying the usual menus, which is important, and not only in the kitchen. They are principally dessert recipes, as simple as could be, because in Germany, as in so many

July 19 1969

Menu

LUNCH

Olives d'Antibes & Komiisbrot

Roast Beef

Insalata di Sedano alla Aldo

Apple sauce maison

Ice Cream • Yoghurt • Cheese cake

Carlsberg Beer

other countries, the dessert is not kept for festive occasions but features in everyday fare.

German cooking is not heavy, as is generally supposed. It is a question of knowing how to choose. Once upon a time in Germany the cooking, like all the other domestic chores, was done at night by the Heizelmenschen, industrious gnomes not unlike Snow White's dwarves. All the womenfolk had to do was not to get up early enough to catch them at their work. Except that one *hausfrau* from Cologne could not resist and got up very early. From that day to this the gnomes have disappeared and are only to be discovered in German cookbooks where they slice, grate, season, knead, pop in the oven and do their tasting armed with forks and ladles that are bigger than they are.

And here is our first gnome, greeting us affably, with a large fork pointed at a notice saying '*Rühr-eier*'.

Scrambled Egg, Frankfurt-style: Rühr-eier

This is a speciality of Frankfurt-on-Main, and is less scrambled than ours in Italy, more Olympian, Goethe-esque.

One egg per person plus one for the pan. Break the eggs into a bowl, add a spoonful of water per egg and a little salt. Whisk with a fork. Fry sufficient butter in the pan until it is well browned. Turn the flame down to a minimum. Toss in the eggs and use a spatula to gently move the part that is setting while you make the still-liquid part run on to the hottest surface of the pan. The knack, for the cook, is to get the eggs to set but only just. The surface should be frothy, like the inside of an omelette.

For an Italian variant you can blend into the egg some grated Parmesan or some tomato sauce, or both; or a light *peperonata*, made of well-cooked peppers and the odd tomato, in which case what you'll have is a sort of Basque *piperade*.

Tatsch

This is a kind of pancake cut into pieces which is often eaten at night with all manner of things: salads, ham, cheese. It is not really a German dish, rather a Swiss one.

For four people: three spoonfuls of flour, a level saltspoon of salt, one teacup of milk, two eggs, a modest 50 g butter.

Blend together the flour, salt and milk, then add the beaten eggs. Melt the butter in a frying pan and pour in the batter, and use your spatula to keep lifting the edges where they stick so that the liquid part comes into contact with the bottom of the pan. When all the mixture is set, cut the pancake into pieces with the spatula and flip them over; then lower the flame and put the lid on the pan for a few minutes so that the mixture cooks and swells.

Remove the lid and cut up the pieces even smaller, turning them over, then cover for a little.

After fifteen minutes remove the lid completely and continue to cut up the *tatsch* and turn it over until you have very small pieces. Stir in a little butter and transfer the *tatsch* to a well-warmed serving dish.

Gnocchi, German-style: Klöse

Klöse means gnocchi (normally small dumplings) and, like gnocchi, it is a generic term that may indicate this and many another type of gnocchi.

For four people: 500 g flour, two teacups of milk, two large eggs, a level saltspoon of salt, a bowl of bread (sandwich-loaf or rolls) cut into small cubes, oil or butter as needed to fry the bread.

For the sauce: 50 g butter, a few spoonfuls of milk, a pinch of salt.

Put a good half of the flour and some of the milk into a bowl and mix with the wooden spoon or, to save labour, with an electric blender. Add the rest of the flour, then the eggs and salt. Keep adding the milk (it may not be necessary to add all of it) so as to keep the dough solid and smooth (beat it with the spoon). This should take about fifteen minutes.

Fry the cubes of bread on a low heat until they are crisp. Mix them into the dough.

Meanwhile you will have brought a saucepan of salted water to the boil, as though to cook spaghetti. Take a metal spoon (preferably one that's a size larger than the standard soup spoon), dip it into the boiling water, take a full spoonful of dough and dip it back into the boiling water until the dumpling (the size of a middling potato) floats to the surface. Continue dropping gnocchi into the saucepan, as fast as you can. The water will go off the boil. Cook for ten minutes from when the water returns to the boil.

While the gnocchi are boiling, prepare the sauce. Warm the butter in a small saucepan. When it is browned (but not black!) add the same amount of milk, and the salt, and turn off the heat.

The diners break their gnocchi into small pieces on their plates, according to the size of their mouths, and pour on the sauce, and someone completes the dish with a generous grinding of black pepper.

If any gnocchi are left over, they can be cut into smallish pieces the next day and fried in butter.

Salsa verde

This green sauce – and I'm a bit hazy about its German origins – would appear to serve as a bridge between Italy (oil and parsley) and Germany (vinegar and sugar). It is, however, different from the usual *salsa verde* in that it takes no notice of several of the excessive standard ingredients: pickled gherkins, garlic, onion, capers, anchovy fillets, breadcrumbs, pine nuts, boiled potato . . . an overabundance which tends to produce a scrambling of flavours, a defect also to be found in certain musical scores that are of needless complexity or, to remain within our field, in too many mixed salads.

Chop the parsley as finely as possible and put it into the sauceboat. Pour on a little olive oil and stir well to ensure the parsley flavour is absorbed by the oil, then complete the sauce with salt, pepper, a good sprinkling of red-wine vinegar, and as much sugar as it takes to sweeten the vinegar. Should the vinegar be on the strong side, add a spot of red wine, which will also prevent the sauce from becoming too thick.

Try *salsa verde* with hot boiled meats, with cold roasts, with cold meatballs, with lightly hard-boiled eggs cut in two (in buttocks, as the Milanese say).

Semolina Pudding: Griessmehlpudding

Semolina pudding should ideally be made with a special coarse-ground semolina which works better than normal semolina, although this will do perfectly well.

For six: 60 g sugar, the grated rind of a lemon, 750 ml milk, 85 g semolina (coarse-ground, ideally) and two eggs.

Put the sugar on a sheet of greaseproof paper, sprinkle the lemon rind over it and mix together. Meanwhile, warm the milk in a saucepan. Add the sugar and lemon-rind mixture. When the milk comes to the boil gently pour in the semolina, stirring with the wooden spoon. Cook for fifteen minutes, stirring frequently until the semolina has swollen up and thickened a little. Take the pan off the stove and stir in the beaten eggs. Return to the stove, and keep stirring. Once the mixture reaches boiling point, the pudding is done. Transfer it into a good oval glazed terracotta mould, brown on the outside and pudding-coloured within, with a bunch of grapes and two vine leaves (optional) scored out; you should keep the mould until this moment brimful of cold water, to ensure that when the pudding is un-moulded it will come out cleanly once it has cooled. The youngest member of the household will have the duty of cleaning off the saucepan and the wooden spoon. Turn the pudding out on to a serving dish. It should be neither too soft nor too firm. It is good served lukewarm or cold. A little raspberry syrup may be poured on top.

Lemon rind is often poisoned by pesticides sprayed on with no regard to the health of those who will eat the lemon. Washing it, in such cases, is useless. The thing is to buy lemons guaranteed free of these poisons, and take them on trust; otherwise just imagine that we are gradually accustoming ourselves to tolerate being poisoned, as tyrants did of old. While we Italians wait for our own Ralph Nader.

Sweet Rice and Milk: Reisbrei

This is a dessert eaten lukewarm or cold: refreshing and light.

For three: a litre of milk, 100 g pudding rice, a small pinch of salt, a heaped spoonful of sugar, a little powdered cinnamon.

Heat the milk. When it comes to the boil add the rice and salt. Keep stirring to prevent the rice from catching. After half an hour (the skin that forms on the milk is absorbed in the course of cooking) add the sugar, stir and leave the mixture to boil for a few more minutes: it should remain relatively liquid. Pour into a fairly shallow dish. Before serving, sprinkle with more sugar and cinnamon.

Apple Pancakes: *Apfelpfannkuchen*

For two or three persons: two apples which, as for an apple tart, need to be juicy and not too sweet, about 30 g butter, a level spoonful of flour, a pinch of salt, half a cup of milk, one egg.

Cut the apples into thick slices (into eight or twelve pieces) and fry them in the butter in a covered pan, on a low heat, until they are tender and browned (about twenty minutes).

Put the flour and salt into a cup. Add half the milk and mix with the wooden spoon, then add the beaten egg. Keep mixing as you add the rest of the milk.

Pour the batter over the apples in the pan (on a low heat) and use the spatula to spread it out. As soon as the batter sets, slide it out on to the pan lid, dot with butter and turn it over. Cover the pan, and still on a low heat, cook for a further five minutes at least, during which time the batter will swell up. Once it has swelled the pancake is ready. Transfer to a serving dish and sprinkle a little sugar on top. Serve hot or cold.

The pancakes may also be made using other fruit: bilberries, currants, strawberries, raspberries, black or red cherries, plums. As these fruits are very juicy the recipe will need slight modification.

Warm the butter, put in the batter. When the batter sets (at that very moment) lay the fruit on top, dust it with crumbled biscuits, add a few dabs of butter, flip over the pancake and keep it covered. The biscuit crumbs together with the juice from the fruit make a delicious crust at the edges of the pan. At the end, turn the pancake once more and slide on to the serving dish with the usual dusting of sugar.

Pauper Knights: Arme Ritter

Knights because they are fried in butter, pauper because they are made with stale bread.

For four: one egg, two spoonfuls of sugar, 500 ml milk, bread (left over from the day before, but not dry; bread rolls are best), as much as is needed to absorb the milk, 50 g butter, sugar and powdered cinnamon to sprinkle on the pudding before serving.

Beat the egg in an earthenware bowl, then stir in the sugar and milk. Slice the bread rolls thickly, as though for a sandwich, then put them into the bowl and leave them long enough to absorb the milk mixture. If there is too much of the mixture, add some more bread, even pieces of irregular shape (irregularity, in the kitchen, is frequently a source of delectation).

Put the butter into a frying pan and fry the pauper knights on both sides. Lift them out of the pan (they should be crisp outside and soft inside) and put them on to a plate; sprinkle them with sugar and cinnamon.

Spekulatius

These are biscuits to be hung by a golden thread
from the Christmas tree – which is not a plastic
object but a dwarf fir tree that actually smells like a
fir. The firs sold to us at Christmas are normally
quite odourless, of no more use than a rose without fragrance. It is, after all, the smell of the tree
which, together with the aroma of the things
hung on it (apples, tangerines, biscuits, nougat,
chocolates) and the wax candles, provides the
delicious scent of Christmas, which nobody for-
gets who has smelt it as a child.

Dressing the tree is a job for the adults of the
household. The children ought to see it once it is
ready, with all the candles lit, as a magical appari-
tion. The apples serve a particular function: with
their weight they pull down the branches, which
tend to rise too high; these therefore are put on
first, to spread out and balance the tree. The
tangerines follow, possibly with their leaves,
and then the other things. Finally (after midnight)
the coloured glass balls and the silver (not aluminium) tinsel are added, and the careful business of dressing the tree is completed with the star

of Bethlehem placed on the very top. The candles, besides giving out their magical golden light, warm the pine needles on the adjacent branches and contribute to producing the Christmas fragrance. Nowadays they are more often than not replaced by multi-coloured electric bulbs which light up and go out with the obsessive rhythm of a neon sign that filters through the half-closed blinds of hotel rooms in crime movies.

For the *Spekulatius* cookies (a normal quantity): 400 g flour, 200 g softened butter, 300 g sugar, two eggs, grated rind of a lemon, a half teaspoon of powdered cinnamon, a small glass of Marsala, a teaspoonful of powdered yeast for desserts.

The dough is prepared the day before so that it may harden.

Put the flour into a bowl. Cut the butter into the flour in small pieces. Add the remaining ingredients, except for the yeast, and continue to blend them, first with a knife, then with your hands, until you have obtained a ball of dough. Keep in the bowl, with a plate on top, in the refrigerator to harden [overnight].

The following day, roll out the dough with a rolling pin on a board. Sprinkle the yeast over it and incorporate it, kneading as little as possible. Then roll out the dough again until it is as thin as a sheet of tagliatelle. Use biscuit cutters to cut out stars, fir trees, rabbits, geese, etc., the size of a tangerine or orange. Or use a sharp knife to cut out the shapes.

Butter two baking sheets, place the *Spekulatius* on them and bake in the oven preheated to 150°C [300°F/gas mark 3] for about fifteen minutes. Once they have browned (but not too much) they are ready. Remove from the oven and free the biscuits at once from the baking sheets with a spatula. They should remain a little soft to the touch on top. When they cool they become crisp.

Cups and Punches: Bowle

The '*Bowle*' is a capacious porcelain receptacle, often highly decorated, a sort of soup tureen with a lid and a large lidded metal spoon, the lid perforated. In the summer it is used in the preparation and serving of a refreshing drink that involves white wine and fruit, fragrant herbs and even cucumber. In German the drink is called a *Bowle*, like its receptacle (from the English word bowl).

The standard household '*Bowle*' is made with peaches, concocted hastily and following no rules.

Peel (or not, as you wish) some ripe peaches, slice them up into a punch bowl (or, following the general decline in standards, into a jug), add a little sugar and pour over them some white wine, something in the order of a Rhenish or Moselle wine, or more simply (a further sacrilege, but never mind) a light red wine. Chill in the refrigerator for a few hours, then serve the wine and (final sacrilege) peach slices. In Tuscany the familiar cup made with oranges (sliced oranges, sugar and wine) used to include white Reno wine from around Bologna, which, strangely enough, worked marvellously well.

Given the excellence of this drink, I give a few recipes for authentic versions.

Peach Cup

Peel the ripe peaches, slice them and put them into the punch bowl in layers, with a sprinkling of sugar on each layer, then a little water to melt it. Cover with greaseproof paper and the lid. Leave to rest in a cool place for at least eight hours. Shortly before serving add the wine.

To give some idea of the size of a punch bowl, the amount of wine to pour in is six to eight bottles. If you wish to use champagne, which of course goes perfectly well, put it in at the very last moment. Serve in crystal tumblers with handles so as not to warm the drink, making use of the spoon with the perforated lid in order to pour the wine while holding back the peach slices.

What is the famous 'Bellini' served in Harry's Bar in Venice if not a peach cup?

Strawberry Cup

This is made the same way as Peach Cup but using wild strawberries. Please note, however: once the strawberries have been put into the bowl with sugar and a little water, shake up the berries in the bowl, rather than mixing them with a spoon, to avoid crushing them.

Lemon Cup

Soak the thinly pared rind of a lemon in 250 ml water for an hour in a cool place. Pour the water through a sieve into the punch bowl, adding the lemon, thinly sliced. Finish with two bottles of Moselle and two of sparkling mineral water, well chilled.

Fragrant Asperula Cup

On the Rhine cruise boats, in May, Waldmeister Cup is served, made with *Asperula odorata* (sweet woodruff), a fragrant herb.

Gather the asperula before they come into flower (little white flowers), pick off the lower leaves, give the herbs a quick rinse, tie them into bunches and place them in the bottom of the punch bowl. Pour the wine on to them and leave it to absorb the flavour of the asperula (which doesn't take long); then remove the bunches and leave the bowl in a cool place, taking care that no leaves have remained in the wine. A slice or two of orange goes well. Thus flavoured, the wine keeps for a long time.

Waldmeister Cup is drunk slowly, while seated on the ship's deck in a cane chair, listening to the song of the Lorelei.

How to Write Out a Recipe

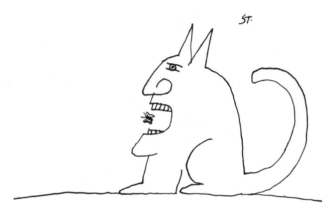

What is the best way to write out a recipe?

To this day no definitive answer has been given to this question.

Should we use the imperative: 'Place the pan on the stove . . .', or the present participle: 'Placing the pan on the stove . . .', or the passive form: 'The pan is placed on the stove . . .', or the first person singular: 'I place the pan on the stove . . .', or the first person plural: 'We place the pan on the stove . . .', or the exhortatory future as used by Gadda: 'You shall place the pan on the stove . . .'?

And as for quantities and timings: mathematical precision: '20 grams (g)', '500 ml', 'seven minutes'; or domestic approximations: 'a knob of butter', 'as needed', 'a cup'? (In Anglo-Saxon recipes the cup is, in fact, a precise measure equivalent to half a pint, that is, a generous 250 ml).[1]

The writer Giuseppe Prezzolini favours the easy-going approximation: 'And, in any case, vague recipes are to be preferred, like those of Artusi, ones expressed thus: a glass of wine . . . (and who's to determine its capacity?), a small pinch of salt . . . (taken with whose fingertips?), half an onion . . . (its size is anyone's guess)'.[2]

The happiest example of imprecision is to be found in a recipe by Maestro Martino, a celebrated fifteenth-century chef from Como, in fact the most illustrious Italian chef of that age.[3] The recipe, possibly too elementary to feature in a high-class cookbook, is for boiled eggs: 'Eggs steeped in their shells', that is, cooked in their shells. 'Put the fresh eggs into cold water and allow them to boil for the duration of a Paternoster or a little longer,' writes Martino, adopting a

[1] Be it noted, however, that the American pint is not the exact equivalent of the British one. (Translator)
[2] Prezzolini's books include *Spaghetti Dinner*, Abelard-Schuman, New York, 1955.
[3] Maestro Martino, *Libro de arte coquinaria composto per lo egregio Maestro Martino coquo olim del reverendissimo monsignor camorlengo et patriarcha de Aquileia.*

unit of time in keeping with his post as chef to the Patriarch of Aquileia, and one which was in common use in those days when clocks were a rare commodity.

A novel way to write out a recipe appeared in the *New Yorker* of 13 January 1975. In a drawing by Edward Koren a lady is to be seen in her kitchen, spoon (wooden, I trust) in hand, in front of a large bowl and an open cookbook. She is reading a recipe.

'In a large bowl mix 60 cents' worth of eggs, 45 cents' worth of cream, 16 cents' worth of oregano, and 10 cents' worth of mustard. Add to this mixture $7.50's worth of pork cutlets and coat them in 65 cents' worth of breadcrumbs. Heat 90 cents' worth of peanut oil in a heavy frying pan and fry the cutlets slowly on 94 cents' worth of gas.'

Como has dedicated a street to Maestro Martino; it is near the ancient Contrada dei Fiori, later called Via Santo Garovaglio, who is not a saint but a nineteenth-century naturalist, a 'happy seeker into nature' following in the footsteps of Pliny the Elder who, with Pliny the Younger, makes up the most ancient pair of illustrious men from Como. (Nowadays the two Plinys, were they still alive, would each of them be almost 2,000 years old, and it would be difficult to tell the Elder and the Younger apart.) To Alessandro Volta, inventor of potato gnocchi as also of the electric battery, Como has even dedicated a temple by the lakeside. . . . But all I wanted to say was simply that Santo

was the name of Professor Commendator Garovaglio (1805–82), known as Santino from his ten-
derest youth. In this street I was born, in a house
that still survives – a blessing not available to many
– precisely as it used to be.

When I lived in Via Santo Garovaglio, Como was
famous for three things: 'el domm, la rana e i tett de
la Besana [the cathedral, the frog and Besana's
breasts]', Besana being a florist who kept her stall
close by the legendary frog carved in a side door of
the cathedral – and she too has in turn become
legendary on account of her splendid bosom.

I step into Via Maestro Martino, an old narrow
street on a slight upward incline, closed off at the
end by the cliff-like Mount Brunate. Here is
the Farmacia Barazzoni, the Caffè Lario, the
Autofficina garage, the Prestino (baker's), the
Montòrfano barber's shop; and finally a restaurant – an ancient trattoria necessarily 'renovated'.

In I go. The place is empty, it being barely
eleven o'clock in the morning; the only activity
is in the kitchen. Who knows, perhaps when I was
small my father, christened Tomaso but generally
known as Paolino, may have taken the family here
to eat one Sunday. At a serving hatch an elderly
coquo, with a white chef's hat on his head, comes
into view; he offers a polite greeting.

I tell him about Martino, who has left a book of
recipes.

'Why not retrieve one or two dishes, follow
the odd suggestion? For instance: on the fried

freshwater shad ('ces petits poissons dont les Comasques sont si fiers,' a friend of Garovaglio would say), 'instead of lemon, Martino suggests a squeeze of orange juice. How about it?'

The old man shakes his tall white hat. 'It's not the season now for shad.'

'What do you think about a street being named after a chef? Doesn't it strike you that this is an intelligent and civilised idea for Como to have hit upon?'

The old man gives another shake of his hat.

'No,' he says. He thinks for a moment then concludes: 'The chef is no different to a serving wench.'

Oh dear! This small consideration a chef has for his profession is depressing, even if it is only a momentary outburst. Returning to his work, the chef invites me to come back when there are shad available, to try them with orange juice.

I leave the restaurant. But I am no longer in Via Maestro Martino. The fact is there is no such street in Como, just as there appears to be no Rue Carême or Escoffier in Paris. No such thing. There is Via Santo Garovaglio, there's the lake, rimmed with floating garbage, the sun, the funicular up the mountainside. But Via Maestro Martino: no.[4]

[4] In fact, a street named after Carême did exist in Paris and was located just where it should be: it cut right through the middle of Les Halles. But it disappeared when this lovely market was pulled down.

Index

A NOTE ON THE AUTHOR

Aldo Buzzi was born in Como in 1910. He is an architect and an essayist who worked in Italian cinema and then for the publisher Rizzoli for many years. Aldo Buzzi lives in Milan.

A NOTE ON THE ARTIST

Saul Steinberg (1914–1999) was one of America's best-loved artists, renowned for the drawings that appeared in the *New Yorker* and for the artwork exhibited internationally in museums and galleries. He and Aldo Buzzi met in architecture school in Milan in the 1930s and remained close friends until Steinberg's death.

A NOTE ON THE TRANSLATOR

Guido Waldman's many translations from the Italian include Ariosto's *Orlando Furioso* and Boccaccio's *Decameron* for the Oxford University Press World Classics series; and Alessandro Baricco's novel *Silk*, for which he was awarded the Weidenfeld Prize.

A NOTE ON THE TYPE

Guardi was designed by Reinhard Haus of Linotype in 1987. It was named after the Guardi brothers, Gianantonio and Francesco, the last famous artists from the Renaissance Venetian school of painting. It is based on the Venetian text styles of the fifteenth century. The influence of characters originally written with a feather can be seen in many aspects of this modern alphabet.